RAY BRADBURY

Ray Bradbury, courtesy of Photofest, Inc.

RAY BRADBURY

A Critical Companion

Robin Anne Reid

CRITICAL COMPANIONS TO POPULAR CONTEMPORARY WRITERS
Kathleen Gregory Klein, Series Editor

Greenwood Press
Westport, Connecticut • London

Library of Congress Cataloging-in-Publication Data

Reid, Robin Anne, 1955–
    Ray Bradbury : a critical companion / Robin Anne Reid.
      p. cm.—(Critical companions to popular contemporary writers, ISSN 1082–4979)
    Includes bibliographical references and index.
    ISBN 0–313–30901–9 (alk. paper)
    1. Bradbury, Ray, 1920—Criticism and interpretation. 2. Science fiction,
American—History and criticism. I. Title. II. Series.
PS3503.R167Z86 2000
813'.54—dc21   00–022332

British Library Cataloguing in Publication Data is available.

Library of Congress Catalog Card Number: 00–022332
ISBN: 0–313–30901–9
ISSN: 1082–4979

First published in 2000

Greenwood Press, 88 Post Road West, Westport, CT 06881
An imprint of Greenwood Publishing Group, Inc.
www.greenwood.com

Printed in the United States of America

The paper used in this book complies with the
Permanent Paper Standard issued by the National
Information Standards Organization (Z39.48–1984).

10 9 8 7 6 5 4 3 2 1

To my grandparents
Ben and Margaret Harris
Max and Hazel Reid

I remember their love
every day of my life.

Contents

Contents

Series Foreword

The authors who appear in the series Critical Companions to Popular Contemporary Writers are all best-selling writers. They do not simply have one successful novel, but a string of them. Fans, critics, and specialist readers eagerly anticipate their next book. For some, high cash advances and breakthrough sales figures are automatic; movie deals often follow. Some writers become household names, recognized by almost everyone.

But, their novels are read one by one. Each reader chooses to start and, more importantly, to finish a book because of what she or he finds there. The real test of a novel is in the satisfaction its readers experience. This series acknowledges the extraordinary involvement of readers and writers in creating a best-seller.

The authors included in this series were chosen by an Advisory Board composed of high school English teachers and high school and public librarians. They ranked a list of best-selling writers according to their popularity among different groups of readers. For the first series, writers in the top-ranked group who had received no book-length, academic, literary analysis (or none in at least the past ten years) were chosen. Because of this selection method, Critical Companions to Popular Contemporary Writers meets a need that is being addressed nowhere else. The success of these volumes as reported by reviewers, librarians, and teachers led to an expansion of the series mandate to include some writers with wide critical attention—Toni Morrison, John Irving, and Maya Angelou, for example—to extend the usefulness of the series.

The volumes in the series are written by scholars with particular expertise in analyzing popular fiction. These specialists add an academic focus to the popular success that these writers already enjoy.

The series is designed to appeal to a wide range of readers. The general reading public will find explanations for the appeal of these well-known writers. Fans will find biographical and fictional questions answered. Students will find literary analysis, discussions of fictional genres, carefully organized introductions to new ways of reading the novels, and bibliographies for additional research. Whether browsing through the book for pleasure or using it for an assignment, readers will find that the most recent novels of the authors are included.

Each volume begins with a biographical chapter drawing on published information, autobiographies or memoirs, prior interviews, and, in some cases, interviews given especially for this series. A chapter on literary history and genres describes how the author's work fits into a larger literary context. The following chapters analyze the writer's most important, most popular, and most recent novels in detail. Each chapter focuses on one or more novels. This approach, suggested by the Advisory Board as the most useful to student research, allows for an in-depth analysis of the writer's fiction. Close and careful readings with numerous examples show readers exactly how the novels work. These chapters are organized around three central elements: plot development (how the story line moves forward), character development (what the reader knows of the important figures), and theme (the significant ideas of the novel). Chapters may also include sections on generic conventions (how the novel is similar to or different from others in its same category of science fiction, fantasy, thriller, etc.), narrative point of view (who tells the story and how), symbols and literary language, and historical or social context. Each chapter ends with an "alternative reading" of the novel. The volume concludes with a primary and secondary bibliography, including reviews.

The alternative readings are a unique feature of this series. By demonstrating a particular way of reading each novel, they provide a clear example of how a specific perspective can reveal important aspects of the book. In the alternative reading sections, one contemporary literary theory—way of reading, such as feminist criticism, Marxism, new historicism, deconstruction, or Jungian psychological critique—is defined in brief, easily comprehensible language. That definition is then applied to the novel to highlight specific features that might go unnoticed or be understood differently in a more general reading. Each volume defines two or three specific theories, making them part of the reader's understanding of how diverse meanings may be constructed from a single novel.

Taken collectively, the volumes in the Critical Companions to Popular Contemporary Writers series provide a wide-ranging investigation of the complexities of current best-selling fiction. By treating these novels seriously as both literary works and publishing successes, the series demonstrates the potential of popular literature in contemporary culture.

Kathleen Gregory Klein
Southern Connecticut State University

Acknowledgments

I owe a special debt to Eileen Reid for her willingness to change a summer vacation into a full-time writing opportunity and for her continued and loving support and sense of humor. Encouragement from Jonathan Eller and William F. Touponce proved to me once again the extent to which academia is a community, and I appreciate their help. I would also like to thank my colleagues at Texas A&M-Commerce, especially Dr. Judy Ann Ford, Dr. James Grimshaw, and Dr. R. N. Singh. My department as a whole continues to acknowledge scholarship in the area of science fiction, and I appreciate their commitment to expanding professional and literary boundaries. For help on research and bibliographic materials, I would like to thank Colin Charlton (and Ian!) for going above and beyond the expected. I would also like to thank Scott Downing for help with interlibrary loans, and the reference librarians and computer support staff in Gee Library. For special help regarding monies and materials, I would like to thank Natalie Henderson and Penny Dooley. Finally, I would like to thank Kathleen Gregory Klein and Lynn Malloy for their feedback throughout the project. Funding for this research was provided in part through an Organized Research Grant from Texas A&M University-Commerce.

1

The Life of Ray Bradbury

Ray Douglas Bradbury was born on August 22, 1920, in Waukegan, Illinois, a town he would later fictionalize as Green Town in numerous stories and several novels. His father, Leonard Spaulding Bradbury, worked as a telephone lineman. His mother was Esther Marie Moberg Bradbury. Bradbury had older twin brothers, Leonard and Samuel, who were born in 1916, and a younger sister, Elizabeth, born in 1926. His brother Samuel died in 1918, and his sister in 1927 (Nolan 39–40).

Bradbury has described his childhood in detail, claiming total recall from birth on. Seeing Lon Chaney in *The Hunchback of Notre Dame* at the age of three profoundly affected him. Memories and images of Chaney as Quasimodo, a deformed man perceived as a monster, strongly inform *A Graveyard for Lunatics*, Bradbury's novel about being a screenwriter in Hollywood. Other childhood passions included "Douglas Fairbanks, Edgar Allan Poe when [he] was eight, Buck Rogers at nine, Tarzan at ten, and all the science fiction magazines from these same years" (Nolan 5). David Mogen, the author of one of the two scholarly monographs on Bradbury's work, argues that Bradbury's "immersion in popular culture" from an early age grew to include a wide variety of media, including "books, comics, movies, theater, museums, magic-shows, circuses," all of which shaped him as a writer (Mogen 2).

Because of ongoing work and economic problems, the Bradbury family moved often, from Waukegan to Arizona and back in 1926–27 and 1932–

33, then to Los Angeles in 1934 (Nolan 43). The family stayed in California long enough for Bradbury to enter Los Angeles High School, where he was active in the drama club and took writing courses (Nolan 45). Bradbury's early interest in acting, which he almost chose as a career, has remained strong throughout his life. He began publishing poetry, short stories, and articles during his high school years. After graduating in 1938, Bradbury continued to live with his family, selling newspapers for ten dollars a week (Nolan 52).

Bradbury's love for both his hometowns, Waukegan (Green Town) and Los Angeles (depicted in *Death Is a Lonely Business* and *A Graveyard for Lunatics* as energetic and creative), comes through in his writing. However, Mogen cites one of Bradbury's stories as well as personal interviews to show that Bradbury's own adolescence was difficult: he wore glasses and was teased by his peers, and found solace in his love for movies. He sought out stars, rollerskating ten miles to the studio to get their autographs (Mogen 5), a story he also tells about his teenage self in *A Graveyard for Lunatics*.

During high school and after, Bradbury was an active science fiction fan, joining the Los Angeles Science Fiction League, where he met Forrest Ackerman, Henry Kuttner, and Ray Harryhausen. All three of these men merit entries in *The Encyclopedia of Science Fiction* for their contributions to the genre: Ackerman published widely in the fan journals and worked as an editor and agent (Clute 3). Kuttner was a writer who published in *Weird Tales* (as would Bradbury) and who later wrote science fiction, publishing under a number of pseudonyms and often collaborating with his wife, C. L. Moore (Clute 682). Ray Harryhausen, the basis for the character of Roy Holdstrom in *A Graveyard for Lunatics*, created special effects for a number of science fiction and fantasy movies such as *The Beast from 20,000 Fathoms* (1953), *The Seventh Voyage of Sinbad* (1958), *Jason and the Argonauts* (1963), and *One Million Years B.C.* (1960) (Clute 548).

Bradbury was active in the "fandom" subculture, groups of science fiction fans who began organizing and publishing amateur magazines known as fanzines. Fandom originated in the late 1920s and grew during the 1940s (Clute 402). Fan groups were the first to organize conventions where writers, editors, and fans could meet to talk about science fiction. Science fiction in America has been characterized by a closeness between writers and their fans, with many fans eventually becoming writers. Bradbury's interest in science fiction led to problems at school, including being "the only student in the fiction class who did *not* get a story printed in the high school short stories anthologies" because he wrote science fiction (Mogen 6).

Bradbury followed the well-trod path from fan to writer: he published stories, cartoons, and columns in other people's fanzines, then began publishing his own mimeographed fanzine in 1939, putting out four issues of *Futuria Fantasia* (Clute 151). He attended the first World Science Fiction Convention, held in New York in 1939. In 1940, Bradbury met Robert Heinlein and attended one of his writing classes. Heinlein is one of the best-known science fiction writers, and is considered one of the major forces in the field from 1940 to 1960 (Clute 554). In 1941, Bradbury met Leigh Brackett, who started to work regularly with him on his stories. Brackett wrote fantasy, science fiction, and mysteries, publishing stories and novels and writing screenplays as well (Clute 150). Bradbury wrote fifty-two stories during 1941 and sold three of them. During that year, he decided to choose writing, rather than acting, as his full-time career, and within a year was able to give up selling newspapers because of the money he made from selling stories (Nolan 52–54).

For his writing Bradbury rented a room in a Los Angeles tenement building. The room, and the friends he made during that time, serve as the basis for the building and characters described in *Death Is a Lonely Business*, and inspired several of his short stories about Mexican Americans. Because of vision problems, Bradbury could not serve during World War II, but he wrote material for the Red Cross and the Civil Defense.

Bradbury met Marguerite Susan McClure in a bookstore in 1946. They began dating, and married in 1947. Between 1949 and 1958, they had four daughters: Susan Marguerite, Ramona Anne, Bettina Francion, and Alexandra Allison. Bradbury continued to support his family through his writing, becoming the only science fiction writer of this period to break into the higher-paying "slick" magazines. As he notes in *Zen in the Art of Writing*, the pulps paid from twenty to forty dollars a story; the sale of forty stories in 1944 earned him eight hundred dollars (68).

Bradbury also wrote and sold mystery and suspense stories, as well as science fiction and horror or "weird" tales. His stories began winning awards outside the science fiction or mystery fields. Bradbury's fiction continued to win literary prizes and anthology publication, and he eventually decided not to write for the cheaper pulp magazines anymore. The late 1940s and 1950s were when much of his best-known work was written and published: *The Martian Chronicles* (1950), *The Illustrated Man* (1951), *Fahrenheit 451* (1953), and *Dandelion Wine* (1957). Several collections of his short stories appeared during the 1950s as well. Bradbury's earliest published work (during the '40s) was highly successful within the genre publications that were read by science fiction and horror fans. His breakthrough to mainstream popularity occurred in 1950 after Christopher Isherwood, a writer and mainstream literary critic, wrote a favorable review of *The Martian Chronicles,* considered by many to be Bradbury's greatest achievement (Mogen 15; Clute 151).

Bradbury also worked on movie scripts. His first movie job was at Universal Studios, where he produced a 110-page film treatment that was made into the first 3-D science fiction movie, *It Came from Outer Space* (Nolan 59). In 1953, director John Huston asked him to write the script for *Moby Dick,* a project that took Bradbury and his family to Ireland for seven months (and which provided him with material for short stories and a novel, *Green Shadows, White Whale*) (Nolan 60). His scriptwriting experiences form the basis of *A Graveyard for Lunatics.* He has continued to write scripts for dramatic and television production, with recent adaptations of his stories appearing on the syndicated television series *Ray Bradbury Theatre* (May 1985–October 1992).

Bradbury continues to write fiction, but he has also written plays, screenplays, and poetry, as well as a book on creative writing and numerous essays. This remarkable outpouring of creative work (which continues to this day) owes much to Bradbury's habit of writing every day, without fail. He has also served as a creative consultant for the World's Fair and for Disney World, designing part of the United States Pavilion for the 1964 New York World's Fair and Spaceship Earth for the Epcot Center (Bradbury *Zen* 64).

Bradbury's popularity with readers has only grown over the years. In his 1986 study, Mogen claims that more than "four million copies of *The Martian Chronicles* have . . . been sold, and Bradbury has become the world's most widely anthologized author, with selections in over 1200 anthologies" (Mogen 13). Nolan lists languages Bradbury's work has been translated into, with a photograph showing twenty-seven foreign-language editions of *The Martian Chronicles* (Nolan 112).

Bradbury has received numerous awards and honors. Besides the awards won by individual short stories and novels, he has also been honored for his career as a whole. In 1977, Bradbury was awarded the World Fantasy Award for Lifetime Achievement, given annually at the World Fantasy Convention. In 1988, the Science Fiction and Fantasy Writers of America (the major professional association of such writers) awarded Bradbury their Grand Master Nebula Award. The Horror

Writers Association (another professional writers' group) awarded Bradbury their major award, the Bram Stoker Award, in three categories in 1989: for a fiction collection (*The Toynbee Convector*), for a short story ("The Thing at the Top of the Stairs"), and the Bram Stoker Award for Lifetime Achievement. Other awards include an Emmy for his teleplay of "The Halloween Tree" and an Oscar nomination for his 1962 animated film *Icarus Montgolfier Wright* (Johnston and Jepson; Clute). Two tributes not made by organizations also show Bradbury's broad influence. The first is the 1991 anthology created by writers who set stories in Bradbury's settings, *The Bradbury Chronicles: Stories in Honor of Ray Bradbury*, edited by William F. Nolan and Martin H. Greenberg (Clute 153). The second tribute came in 1971, when the *Apollo 15* crew named a lunar feature Dandelion Crater in honor of Bradbury's work (Nolan 69).

Bradbury currently lives in Los Angeles, writes every day, and habitually works on several projects at a time. He lectures on a regular basis, but is primarily focused on keeping a regular writing schedule.

SOME WORKS CONTAINING BIOGRAPHICAL INFORMATION

Although no biography of Ray Bradbury, as biography is conventionally understood, has been published, one important biographical source where any discussion of Bradbury's life must begin is *The Ray Bradbury Companion* by William F. Nolan. The subtitle of this 1975 work explains its purpose: *A Life and Career History, Photolog, and Comprehensive Checklist of Writings with Facsimiles from Ray Bradbury's Unpublished and Uncollected Work in All Media*. Nolan, a longtime friend of Bradbury, provides a chronological listing of important dates and events, a treasure of photographs and facsimiles, and a comprehensive checklist of Bradbury's writings to that time. The checklist is organized by genre and arranged chronologically.

The fact that Bradbury's own introduction, Nolan's preface, the photographs, and the chronology of Bradbury's life take up only ninety-six pages of a book that is over 320 pages long reveals the extent to which writing makes up a huge part of Bradbury's life. Bradbury's advice to writers to write every day is based on his own experience, since he has always written for hours every day. In the introduction to Nolan's book, Bradbury lists writing as one of his grand passions. Bradbury's identification of his passions also makes it clear that his writing is connected to what he loves: his self-described "obsessions with Space, with magic, with Dracula at midnight and Frankenstein at noon" (Nolan 5).

The other place for readers to search for information on Bradbury's life is in his collections, novels, and other published work. Such information is found in two places: in introductions or afterwords to his fiction and within the stories or novels themselves. In later editions of his fiction, Bradbury provides introductions written sometimes decades after original publication (when the original publishers probably scorned the idea of introductions by mere science fiction writers). These introductions often talk about his writing process and his life. Several of these introductions, along with other essays, have been collected in *Zen in the Art of Writing: Releasing the Creative Genius within You*, Bradbury's 1990 book of advice for writers.

Another place to find information about the writer's life, although readers must approach this source with care, is at the heart of the stories themselves. Of special interest are those works Mogen calls "autobiographical fantasies," in which Bradbury explores and recreates his memories of his childhood and young adulthood. Since Bradbury, as a writer, makes it clear that a great deal of his writing is based to some extent on his own life, an understanding of his life can aid readers in thinking about the writing. However, readers must be careful not to assume a one-to-one relationship between the life of the writer and the fictional work. As Mogen points out, Bradbury alters "the actual facts of his life," often to emphasize a greater connection with "American experience in general" (Mogen 114). One example of alteration Mogen gives is how Bradbury, who was eight in 1928, makes the character of Doug Spaulding twelve in 1928 in order to link the protagonist's growing maturity with the country's economic crash in *Dandelion Wine*.

In a more extended discussion, Wayne L. Johnson, author of the other book on Bradbury's work, describes how Waukegan, where Bradbury was born and lived as a child, was altered in Bradbury's fictional Green Town. The "houses have been romanticized and embellished in the Green Town stories," so that readers who visit Waukegan and expect to see "stately, Victorian style structures, replete with turret-like cupolas and bristling with wrought-iron lightning rods" will be disappointed. The reality is "modest, unadorned frame buildings" (Johnson 90). The ravine, however, more than lives up to the image that Bradbury creates. Johnson argues that "Green Town represents a distillation of Bradbury's experience," a location where Bradbury is free to explore "people, places, and happenings" in ways that could never happen in real life (Johnson 91).

2

Ray Bradbury and the Question of "Science Fiction"

The question of what genre, or genres, Ray Bradbury writes in is a complicated one to answer. A. James Stupple, an academic critic writing in the 1980 Greenberg and Olander anthology, declares that "Bradbury is primarily a science fiction writer" (Stupple "The Past" 30). However, in his 1980 essay, "The Fiction of Ray Bradbury: Universal Themes in Midwestern Settings," Thomas P. Linkfield, an academic critic, claims that, "although most people [associate] Ray Bradbury's name with science fiction, due to the success of *The Martian Chronicles* and other stories dealing with space, a large proportion of his work has nothing whatsoever to do with either space or science fiction" (Linkfield 94).

Another academic critic distinguishes Bradbury from other writers of science fiction. Calvin Miller, in "Ray Bradbury: Hope in a Doubtful Age," argues that Bradbury is an science fiction writer who is better (less silly) than the other science fiction writers. Reading Bradbury, Miller reports that instead of "ray guns, interplanetary wars, and glass-domed demons," he found "real people and circumstances which, while only mildly scientific, soared far above what I expected from science fiction," and which included an "enthralling sense of cosmic spirituality" (Miller 93).

Ultimately, the question of genre depends on what Bradbury works the critic reads. Wayne L. Johnson, in his 1980 book *Ray Bradbury*, arranges his chapters around important themes he finds in Bradbury's work: "Medicines for Melancholy," "The Pandemonium Shadow Show," "Future Imperfect," "Machineries of Joy and Sorrow," "Green Town, Illinois," "Mars," "Other Themes," and "Other Works." David Mogen, in his 1986 book also titled *Ray Bradbury*, focuses individual chapters on Bradbury's pulp magazine publication, "weird tales," space colonization fiction, *The Martian Chronicles*, future warning tales about technology, autobiographical fantasy, realist fiction, and detective fiction, and finishes with a portmanteau chapter focusing on Bradbury's work in film, drama, and poetry.

Bradbury himself addresses the question of whether or not he writes "science fiction" in various places. In the introduction he wrote for *The Ray Bradbury Companion*, he discusses how hard it is for readers born during or after the 1950s to understand what it was like in 1949: "We so-called science fiction writers have always had doubts about that rather dubious label. Mainly because gangs of intellectual apes have clubbed us for a full lifetime, and when they weren't beating us were busily ignoring us. . . . Naturally, most of us grew up with at least a twinge of self-doubt and inferiority" (Nolan 7). Bradbury eloquently describes the marginalization of science fiction readers and writers in the years before the first manned flight to the Moon, which occurred in 1969. That flight, the reality of which made the "fantasies" science fiction had written about for decades exist, changed many people's perception of science fiction.

He also discusses the problem of "science fiction" as a marketing label. When *The Martian Chronicles* was published by Doubleday, the phrase "Doubleday Science Fiction" appeared on the front and back cover. Bradbury notes that this labeling meant "instant neglect for any book so published, so weighted down and intellectually wounded" (Nolan 8)— referring here to critical neglect, the attention of reviewers and academics, not necessarily neglect by readers. In his essay, "Dusk in the Robot Museums: The Rebirth of the Imagination," included in his *Zen in the Art of Writing*, Bradbury writes with glee of the way children led the way to change. In this 1980 praise song for science fiction as *the* literature of ideas, the "Double Revolution in reading, in teaching Literature and pictorial Art," Bradbury claims that the young have raised the flag against the snobbish intellectuals who deride science fiction as popular and thus unworthy of reading (97–107).

The definition of science fiction and the status of this genre, not to mention its ever-growing manifestations in other media such as films and computer games, have changed dramatically in the fifty-plus years since Bradbury published his first novel. However, Bradbury's work has never gone out of fashion: a new computer game based on *The Martian Chronicles* has recently been released.

Bradbury has been active in science fiction fandom, including publishing his own fanzine and attending conventions. In 1952, Bradbury attended "Westercon," a west coast science fiction convention, as the guest of honor, and was elected president of a new group, Science Fiction and Fantasy Writers of America (Nolan 59). As Bradbury's work makes clear, he had more problems with the label of science fiction, and perhaps with people's narrow definition of the genre, than with the freedoms the genre afforded him as a writer. He has included fantastic elements in his work written in other genres, apparently enjoying confounding the critics by mixing genre conventions.

Debate over whether Bradbury should be called a science fiction writer hinges on the various definitions of science fiction, which range from an insistence on careful extrapolation from contemporaneous scientific knowledge to a casual assumption that anything with space ships qualifies as science fiction, as well as the changing sociocultural world in which Bradbury as well as his critics and readers live. The most sustained analysis of Bradbury's changing status is found in Mogen's book, the second chapter of which is titled "Bradbury and the Critics: Between Two Worlds." Mogen traces how Bradbury moved from a genre writer publishing solely in pulp magazines to attaining the mainstream status that he continues to hold today. His popularity, shown by the fact that most of his work has remained in print for decades, has been accompanied by a growing reputation among academic critics.

Mogen notes the paradoxical and controversial history of responses to Bradbury, including the idea that "the most severe criticism of his work has come from the science-fiction community rather than from the mainstream literary establishment. Though he may be the world's best-known science-fiction personality, Bradbury's reputation within the science-fiction community itself has always been ambivalent" (Mogen 14). Mogen quotes the 1978 *Reader's Guide to Science Fiction*, whose editors characterized Bradbury as a "bit of a problem," noting (like Mogen) the different perceptions of Bradbury held by readers, critics, and the science fiction community. This reference work repeats a common criticism of Bradbury's work: that it is "anti-science fiction."

According to Mogen, Bradbury's movement into mainstream publication was marked by more numerous reviews by mainstream writers and reviewers and by increasing sales to the "slick" mainstream magazines, so called because of the quality of their paper, in contrast to the cheaper paper used in the smaller "pulp" magazines. Unfortunately, the mainstream critical praise of Bradbury often involved insulting the quality of all other science fiction, which in turn provoked hostile responses from science fiction writers and critics. Bradbury's success might have indicated the possibility of similar success for other science fiction writers, but some science fiction critics did not appreciate science fiction being defined for mainstream audiences by one writer's work, especially when that work was perceived by some science fiction writers and critics to be non-representative of much of the work published in the genre.

Mogen describes how some writers wanted to define science fiction by criteria established by John W. Campbell, editor of *Astounding Science Fiction* during the 1940s and 1950s, a period often called the golden age of science fiction. The key element of good science fiction, according to Campbell, is a world plausibly extrapolated from, and not contradicting, contemporary scientific knowledge and principles. Science fiction that follows Campbell's principles is sometimes called "hard science fiction" to distinguish it from other subgenres of science fiction such as horror, fantasy, space opera, or science fantasy. Bradbury has "violated" and continues to violate the standards of hard science fiction because he is interested in other ways of writing about the world, the universe, and the human condition.

After summarizing the various debates about Bradbury's status, Mogen provides a "defense." He notes that an examination of Bradbury's work as a whole proves he is not simply against science and technology, but is part of an important science fiction tradition that includes writers such as H. G. Wells, Aldous Huxley, Frederick Pohl, and Ursula K. Le Guin, who "warn about consequences of misusing the new powers" (Mogen 22) and who question the belief that technology always improves life. Mogen argues that Bradbury, as a writer, enjoys contradictions and confounding people: While Bradbury may be against cars, airplanes, telephones, and television, he is a passionate advocate of trains, rockets, movies, radio drama, and comic strips. Mogen argues that while Bradbury's work might not include "the detailed extrapolative dimension and the no-nonsense, world-conquering ethos many science-fiction readers value," part of the problem is caused by "limitations in the aesthetic principles applied by reviewers and critics in the science-fiction field" (Mogen 24).

A further development in the reception of Bradbury's work came about in the 1960s, when Bradbury's work began appearing in literary anthologies published for use in public schools. In 1968, *College English* included a critical study of *Fahrenheit 451*, initiating the growth of academic critical scholarship devoted to Bradbury (Nolan 67). Bradbury notes the nature of this change when he argues that children's love for science fiction and the social revolution of the 1960s led to a more inclusive curriculum that resulted in high schools and colleges teaching more science fiction (Nolan 9). Bringing Bradbury into the schools, Mogen argues, led critics to focus on the artistry of Bradbury's science fiction and the speculative nature and themes of his work, rather than how well the stories met the criteria of scientific extrapolation.

Other academic critics have begun to show the ways in which Bradbury's work is part of an American literary tradition. Mortin I. Teicher, in "Ray Bradbury and Thomas Wolfe: Fantasy and the Fantastic," analyzes the extent to which Bradbury connects his work to reality by incorporating writers as characters into his stories, including Herman Melville, Edgar Allan Poe, Charles Dickens, George Bernard Shaw, Emily Dickinson, Nathaniel Hawthorne, William Shakespeare, and, especially, Thomas Wolfe (Teicher 17). Academic critic Steven Kagle, in "Homage to Melville: Ray Bradbury and the Nineteenth-Century American Romance," situates Bradbury's work firmly in the genre of prose romance: "When we finally try to categorize Ray Bradbury's place as a writer, we will ultimately place him beside Herman Melville and Stephen King rather than Jules Verne and Arthur C. Clarke" (Kagle 279). Kagle argues against working with the popular concept of science fiction (future events set in space), or with Campbell's definition of science fiction as fiction based on extrapolation from known scientific facts. Since Bradbury grew up reading the pulp magazines before those standards were established, what he came to write was "science fantasy," a genre that looks back to a literary tradition that differs from the realistic novel. Kagle places Bradbury in that nineteenth-century tradition, that of Melville and Hawthorne, rather than in the twentieth-century science fiction tradition, since his fiction "does not attempt to adhere to either the scientific or psychological laws of our world" (Kagle 285).

Hazel Pierce, an academic critic, in "Ray Bradbury and the Gothic Tradition," also takes this perspective, arguing that much of Bradbury's work can be understood by studying the conventions of literary genres other than twentieth-century science fiction. She warns that it is dangerous to try to "connect a contemporary author with any established literary tradition" because it is difficult to tell how much of a work is attributable to the influence of the source or genre traditions and what is original from the author (Pierce 165). She quotes Bradbury in an interview where he was posed an either-or question: Do authors invent ideas or "tap" sources? Bradbury presented a synthesis: he sees the "author's purpose [as finding] fresh ways of presenting basic truths" (Pierce 165). Pierce analyzes three of his books (*The October Country*, *Something Wicked This Way Comes*, and *The Halloween Tree*) as examples of Bradbury working within the gothic tradition while simultaneously changing it.

The gothic novel originated in Europe and was revived in the eighteenth century, appearing in architecture as well as literature, which was even then considered "popular" in the derogatory sense. Specifically, the literature was seen as appealing to the common people, the lower class, rather than the intellectual or social elites. Gothic literary conventions include historical settings, particularly castles or churches, and hauntings. Female writers refined the gothic heroine, a virtuous female victim often threatened by erotic decadence. In America, Hawthorne and Poe translated some of the conventions to a fresh setting, blending in more horror (Pierce 167–169). Pierce argues that Poe is the link between Bradbury and the gothic tradition, which depends on such themes as fear of the unknown and the balance between good and evil shown in terms of light and dark.

Pierce examines how Bradbury has used some of the conventions of the gothic while adding his own ideas. For example, Bradbury's stories tend to show innocent young boys rather than women. The light–dark polarity is maintained, as well as the sense of landscape, the "October Country" so familiar to Bradbury's readers. Supernatural elements (Tom Fury, the carnival people in *Something Wicked This Way Comes*), storms, and a kind of "American castle"—the public library—all appear in Bradbury's work, resulting in a new blend of "ancient" and "modern" conventions (Pierce 185).

Bradbury has recently begun publishing novels that blend the conventions of mystery, horror, and suspense with fantastic elements, all drawing on events from his own life as a young writer: *Death Is a Lonely Business* and *A Graveyard for Lunatics*. In these novels, Bradbury uses conventions from the mystery and horror genres, but his fantastic and autobiographical elements tend to result in work that critics do not usually categorize as mystery. Additionally, the problem of marketing still exists: copies of these novels are usually found in science fiction sections of bookstores, not in the mystery sections. Despite his complaints, Bradbury's works will probably continue to be shelved in the science fiction sections of bookstores for some time.

Regardless of how critics—or booksellers—categorize Bradbury's work, or whatever part of it they are choosing to examine, they all agree on the extent to which Bradbury's style identifies him. His style exhibits a lyricism that is sometimes his strength, sometimes his weakness. His lyricism is sometimes evocative, powerful and chilling, and other times is overstated or overly sentimental. Sarah-Warner J. Pell, one of several academic critics who have written on Bradbury's style, has analyzed the imagery in Bradbury's fiction, and Donald Watt analyzes the symbolism in *Fahrenheit 451* (Greenberg and Olander). Mogen also analyzes the influences on Bradbury's style, tracing both the pulp and literary influences, how he moved from imitating the writers around him to develop a "poetry of the unconscious" by focusing on recovering personal memories, and how voracious reading (American literature, Shakespeare, women writers) has shaped his work as well. Mogen also notes the extent to which Bradbury's device of creating asides within his stories (the poetic, metaphorical descriptions that interrupt plots) became a major aspect of his work (Mogen 38–39). The asides, the climactic descriptive moments that often establish major themes, are often what stay in readers' minds.

William F. Touponce, in *Ray Bradbury and the Poetics of Reverie*, analyzes Bradbury's work in the context of phenomenology, a philosophy that "takes as its starting point the world as experienced in our consciousness" (Hawthorn 148). Touponce's ambitious analysis (recently issued in a second edition) starts by assuming the importance of the aesthetic experience with regard to fantasy and science fiction and argues for the importance of Bradbury's use of reverie—daydreams, asides, evocations of memory, and imagination. Touponce's extended and complex reading focuses on the relation between Bradbury's style, the use of reverie, and the magical or fantastic aspects of the work.

OVERVIEW OF MAJOR PUBLICATIONS

Since he first began publishing in fan magazines in the late 1930s, Bradbury has written poetry, short stories, novels, children's books, juveniles, plays, essays, radio scripts, screenplays, and dramatizations of his fiction. He has written horror, suspense, mystery, and science fantasy stories of his own, as well as editing collections of fiction.

In an "Annotated Finding List" that covers Bradbury's short fiction published between 1938 and 1991, Jonathan Eller, a scholar who has done extensive bibliographic scholarship on Bradbury's work, lists 327 "dis-

tinct stories" from "23 major collections [that] have evolved into three
novels . . . [and] have been reprinted in periodicals nearly 450 times"
(Eller "Finding List" 28). Eller claims that "nearly every popular horror,
mystery, and science fiction magazine of the last fifty years has printed
at least one Bradbury story, as have many of the mainstream newspapers
and magazines in America, Canada, and England," and that Bradbury's
stories have appeared "in men's magazines, women's magazines, and
family magazines . . . [as well as] many educational journals" (Eller
"Finding List" 28).

Mogen traces the changes in Bradbury's fiction over the decades: moving from his science fiction and fantasy in the 1940s and early 1950s, to
the "autobiographical fantasy (or fantastical autobiography)" of the later
1950s and early 1960s (Mogen 113), and on to mystery/detective novels
in the 1980s and 1990s (Mogen 11). Bradbury has also published more
poetry and been involved more with drama since the 1960s, and has also
written and published nonfiction articles and essays on a variety of top-
ics (Mogen 12). What follows can only begin to summarize the scope and
richness of Bradbury's written contributions to American literature.

Nonfiction

Nolan's *Bradbury Companion* lists the following kinds of nonfiction:
"Articles and Miscellaneous Non-Fiction" (including essays, commentary, autobiographical sketches, guest columns, and tributes), introductions, reviews, published speeches, published letters, and interviews.
Bradbury has written extensively on all his areas of interest, including
science fiction (writers, fans, and conventions), writing, magic, space
travel, travel on Earth, film, spirituality, censorship, and public trans-
portation. Apparently, only one collection of Bradbury essays, *Zen in the
Art of Writing*, has been published.

Zen brings together previously published articles and two pieces written for the collection. The articles were published in *Writers Digest Books*,
The Writer, other advice books on writing genre fiction, or as introductions to Bradbury's novels (specifically, *Fahrenheit 451* and *Dandelion
Wine*). The articles share a common theme: would-be writers should join
effort with passion. Writers need to write constantly and daily (he rec-
ommends writing a story a week for years) to learn their craft, and they
need to write about their lives with joy and the desire to learn. Because
Bradbury's advice is backed up with examples from his own life and

writing, the collection is useful both for those interested in how Bradbury writes as well as for aspiring writers.

Short Fiction

Bradbury's short stories have been organized in various collections, many of which anthologize stories that appeared in earlier volumes. As later chapters show, critics sometimes disagree on whether specific books are novels or story collections. Books that are given thematic unity through extensive revision of short stories and through bridge chapters (such as *The Martian Chronicles* and *The Illustrated Man*) are included in the Novels section below.

Dark Carnival (1947), published by Arkham House, is a collection of short stories, many of which had been published in *Weird Tales*, a pulp magazine specializing in horror, adventure, and supernatural stories. Although this collection is out of print (just about the only Bradbury book that is), fifteen of Bradbury's favorite stories from *Dark Carnival*, rewritten and combined with others, were later published in *The October Country*. Most of the stories in the original collection, according to Bradbury's comments in the later one, were written before 1946 and before he was twenty-six years old. These stories are more horror and fantasy than science fiction, "weird tales" being more concerned with describing the effects of supernatural events than in creating plausible explanations for them.

The Golden Apples of the Sun (1953) is a collection that mixes both realistic and fantastic stories and contains eighteen stories originally published between 1945 and 1953. The stories are: "The Fog Horn," "The Pedestrian," "The April Witch," "The Wilderness," "The Fruit at the Bottom of the Bowl," "Invisible Boy," "The Flying Machine," "The Murderer," "The Golden Kite, The Silver Wind," "I See You Never," "Embroidery," "The Big Black and White Game," "The Sound of Thunder," "The Great Wide World Over There," "Powerhouse," "En La Noche," "Sun and Shadow," "The Meadow," "The Garbage Collector," "The Great Fire," "Hail and Farewell," and "The Golden Apples of the Sun." "The Big Black and White Game" was sold to *American Mercury* in 1945 and was selected for the *Best American Short Stories* in 1945 (Nolan 55). "Powerhouse" won an O. Henry Award in 1948 (Nolan 57). "I See You Never" was printed in *Best American Short Stories 1948* (Nolan 57). A new trade edition published in 1990 by Avon, titled *The Golden Apples of the*

Sun and Other Stories, combines eighteen of the original twenty-two with fourteen stories from *R Is for Rocket*. This collection presents, again, a blend of genres: science fantasy, fantasy, and supernatural or horror fiction, along with Bradbury's stories that present more realistic characters in stories about American race relations ("The Big Black and White Game") or American tourists in Mexico ("Sun and Shadow").

The October Country (1955) is a collection of gothic, supernatural, and horror stories that includes fifteen revised stories from his first collection, *Dark Carnival*, along with four new ones. The book's epigraph is Bradbury's explanation of the title: The "October Country" is "that country where it is always turning late in the year. . . . where the hills are fog and the rivers are mist. . . . whose people are the autumn people, thinking only autumn thoughts." The nineteen stories are: "The Dwarf," "The Next in Line," "The Watchful Poker Chip of H. Matisse," "Skeleton," "The Jar," "The Lake," "The Emissary," "Touched with Fire," "The Small Assassin," "The Crowd," "Jack-in-the-Box," "The Scythe," "Uncle Einar," "The Wind," "The Man Upstairs," "There Was an Old Woman," "The Cistern," "Homecoming," and "The Wonderful Death of Dudley Stone." "Homecoming" was selected for the O. Henry *Prize Stories of 1947* (Nolan 56). The world of this collection of stories is one dominated by the fear of death and populated with grotesque figures of Halloween or carnival. The concept of the "October Country," the autumn country, informs his later work.

A Medicine for Melancholy (1959) is a collection containing more of Bradbury's realistic stories (some of the ones featuring Mexican Americans and the Irish), with stories that focus on characters gaining new appreciation for the world or their own pasts, with some fantasy and horror. The stories in this collection are: "In a Season of Calm Weather," "The Dragon," "A Medicine for Melancholy," "The Wonderful Ice Cream Suit," "Fever Dream," "The Marriage Mender," "The Town Where No One Got Off," "A Scent of Sarsaparilla," "Icarus Montgolfier Wright," "The Headpiece," "Dark They Were, and Golden-Eyed," "The First Night of Lent," "The Time of Going Away," "All Summer in a Day," "The Gift," "The Great Collision of Monday Last," "The Little Mice," "The Shore Line at Sunset," "The Strawberry Window," and "The Day It Rained Forever." "The Day It Rained Forever" was published in the 1953 *Best American Short Stories* (Nolan 62). Avon Books reissued a 1990 trade paperback edition that contains nineteen stories from the original *Medicine for Melancholy* plus fourteen stories from *S Is for Space* and one excerpt from *Something Wicked This Way Comes*. *Medicine for Melancholy* was combined with *The Golden Apples of the Sun* and issued as *Twice 22* in 1966.

The Machineries of Joy (1964) comprises twenty-one stories, including stories about a Martian, the conflict between a film producer and a special effects man who makes dinosaurs, the Irish, the end of television bringing a better world, the coming of Europeans to the New World (told from the perspective of a grandfather and grandson who see the ship arrive), as well as Mexican stories and various horror stories. The titles in this collection are: "The Machineries of Joy," "The One Who Waits," "Tyrannosaurus Rex," "The Vacation," "The Drummer Boy of Shiloh," "Boys! Raise Giant Mushrooms in *Your* Cellar!," "Almost the End of the World," "Perhaps We Are Going Away," "And the Sailor, Home from the Sea," "El Día de Muerte," "The Illustrated Woman," "Some Live Like Lazarus," "A Miracle of Rare Device," "And So Died Riabouchinska," "The Beggar on O'Connell Bridge," "Death and the Maiden," "A Flight of Ravens," "The Best of All Possible Worlds," "The Lifework of Juan Diaz," "To the Chicago Abyss," and "The Anthem Sprinters."

The Vintage Ray Bradbury (1965) is a collection containing Bradbury's "own selection of his best stories," and includes: "The Watchful Poker Chip of H. Matissse," "The Veldt," "Hail and Farewell," "A Medicine for Melancholy," "The Fruit at the Bottom of the Bowl," "Ylla," "The Little Mice," "The Small Assassin," "The Anthem Sprinters," "And the Rock Cried Out," "Invisible Boy," "Night Meeting," "The Fox and the Forest," "Skeleton," four sections from *Dandelion Wine* ("Illumination," "Dandelion Wine," "Statues," and "Green Wine for Dreaming"), "Kaleidoscope," "Sun and Shadow," "The Illustrated Man," "The Fog Horn," "The Dwarf," "Fever Dream," "The Wonderful Ice Cream Suit," and "There Will Come Soft Rains."

I Sing the Body Electric! (1960) contains eighteen stories, many of which focus on Bradbury's concern with the past and what changes occur as we move into the future (Stupple 32–33). The title story is about a robot grandmother who comes to live with a family after the mother dies. Other stories are set on Mars, or are Bradbury's evocation of some of his favorite writers (Hemingway, Dickens) or historical figures (Lincoln). The stories in this collection are: "The Kilimanjaro Device," "The Terrible Conflagration up at the Place," "Tomorrow's Child," "The Women," "The Inspired Chicken Motel," "Downwind from Gettysburg," "Yes, We'll Gather at the River," "The Cold Wind and the Warm," "Night Call, Collect," "The Haunting of the New," "I Sing the Body Electric!," "The

Tombling Day," "Any Friend of Nicholas Nickelby's is a Friend of Mine," "Heavy-Set," "The Man in the Rorschach Shirt," "Henry the Ninth," "The Lost City of Mars," and "Christus Apollo." Avon published a trade paperback in 1998 with the original stories plus eleven from *Long after Midnight* and *The Stories of Ray Bradbury*.

Long after Midnight (1976) contains twenty-two stories, ranging from autobiographical fantasies to Martian stories, Irish stories, and stories about writers. The stories in this collection are: "The Blue Bottle," "One Timeless Spring," "The Parrot Who Met Papa," "The Burning Man," "A Piece of Wood," "The Messiah," "G.B.S.—Mark V," "The Utterly Perfect Murder," "Punishment without Crime," "Getting through Sunday Somehow," "Drink Entire: Against the Madness of Crowds," "Interval in Sunlight," "A Story of Love," "The Wish," "Forever and the Earth," "The Better Part of Wisdom," "Darling Adolf," "The Miracles of Jamie," "The October Game," "The Pumpernickel," "Long after Midnight," and "Have I Got a Chocolate Bar for You!"

The Stories of Ray Bradbury (1980) is a collection of Bradbury's one hundred favorite stories (Mogen 174). *A Memory of Murder* (1984) is a collection of early short stories that were printed in pulp detective magazines (Mogen 148). According to Mogen, Bradbury introduces the stories, which were written during the 1940s, as perhaps being more of "historical interest" (Mogen 149). This collection preceded Bradbury's first full-length mystery novel (*Death Is a Lonely Business*) (discussed in chapter 8), and Mogen argues that the stories are of interest to Bradbury readers because they share with the novel the strengths of "vivid description, haunting atmosphere, and flamboyant characterization" (Mogen 149).

The Toynbee Convector (1988) contains twenty-three stories including time travel stories, Irish stories, horror stories, and Mars stories. This collection includes: "The Toynbee Convector," "Trapdoor," "On the Orient, North," "One Night in Your Life," "West of October," "The Last Circus," "The Laurel and Hardy Love Affair," "I Suppose You Are Wondering Why We Are Here?," "Lafayette, Farewell," "Banshee," "Promises, Promises," "The Love Affair," "One for His Lordship, and One for the Road!," "After Midnight, in the Month of June," "Bless Me, Father, for I Have Sinned," "By the Numbers!," "A Touch of Petulance," "Long Division," "Come, and Bring Constance!," "Junior," "The Tombstone," "The Thing at the Top of the Stairs," and "Colonel Stonesteel's Genuine Home-Made Truly Egyptian Mummy."

Quicker Than the Eye (1996) contains twenty-one stories, twelve of which were published in 1994–95. The stories include an autobiographical fantasy related to the birth of Bradbury's first child, horror stories, circus or carnival stories, and time travel stories. The stories are "Underseaboat Doktor," "Zaharoff/Richter Mark V," "Remember Sascha?," "Another Fine Mess," "The Electrocution," "Hopscotch," "The Finnegan," "That Woman on the Lawn," "The Very Gentle Murders," "Quicker Than the Eye," "Dorian in Excelsus," "No News, or What Killed the Dog?," "The Witch Door," "The Ghost in the Machine," "At the End of the Ninth Year," "Bug," "Once More, Legato," "Exchange," "Free Dirt," "Last Rites," and "The Other Highway." Bradbury's afterword, titled "Make Haste to Live," gives the original ideas for many of the stories in this collection.

Driving Blind (1997), dedicated to Bradbury's eight grandchildren, contains twenty-one stories, only four of which were published earlier. The stories cross a range of genres, but most seem to focus on intensely emotional relationships, from a dead man who returns to complain about the lack of grief and attention paid to his grave to a moment of sexual intimacy shared between cousins on the occasion of a relative's death. Other stories involve the return of love letters from a long-ago past, a curious friendship between a young boy and a man who wears a sack over his head, and a man returning to a place that was important to him twenty years earlier. Seventeen of the stories have their first publication in this collection, which includes: "Night Train to Babylon," "If MGM Is Killed, Who Gets the Lion?," "Hello, I Must Be Going," "House Divided," "Grand Theft," "Remember Me?," "Fee Fie Foe Fum," "Driving Blind," "I Wonder What's Become of Sally," "Nothing Changes," "That Old Dog Lying in the Dust," "Someone in the Rain," "Madame *et* Monsieur Shill," "The Mirror," "End of Summer," "Thunder in the Morning," "The Highest Branch on the Tree," "A Woman Is a Fast-Moving Picnic," "Virgin Resusitas," "Mr. Pale," and "The Bird That Comes Out of the Clock." An afterword describes the genesis of several of the stories, along with a description of a dream Bradbury once had of driving along with his muse, he in the passenger seat, the muse "driving blind" but knowing all the time where she is going.

Novels

The Martian Chronicles (1950), discussed in chapter 3, arguably remains one of Bradbury's two best known and most influential works (the other being *Fahrenheit 451*). *TMC* was also the book that brought Bradbury's work into the mainstream, due in part to Christopher Isherwood's glow-ing review. Bradbury relates how he developed the work: his interest in Sherwood Anderson's *Winesburg, Ohio* (1919), a longer work that focused on the separate stories of characters within a town, led him to wonder about the possibility of developing a similar collection about Mars. An editor's suggestion that he put his Mars stories into a novel format in-spired him to select and rewrite earlier stories and write a number of new bridging stories for the longer work.

The book is structured around the chronological history of human col-onization of Mars, describing the first explorations, the dying out of the indigenous Martians, the building of human settlements, and the colo-nists' withdrawal after nuclear war breaks out on Earth. Although the use of rockets to colonize Mars is a convention of science fiction, Brad-bury was not concerned with drawing on contemporary scientific knowl-edge about Mars, and his stories are more science fantasy than science fiction.

The Illustrated Man (1951), discussed in chapter 4, includes work in several different genres—science fiction, horror, and fantasy. Bradbury collected short stories published between 1947 and 1950, wrote some new ones, and created a framing story about an unnamed narrator's encoun-ter with an "Illustrated Man" whose tattoos come alive in the dark. As the evening progresses, the narrator sees eighteen tales played out on the Illustrated Man's skin. The eighteen stories are: "The Veldt," "Kalei-doscope," "The Other Foot," "The Highway," "The Man," "The Long Rain," "The Rocket Man," "The Fire Balloons," "The Last Night of the World," "The Exiles," "No Particular Night or Morning," "The Fox and the Forest," "The Visitor," "The Concrete Mixer," "Marionettes, Inc.," "The City," "Zero Hour," and "The Rocket." "The Other Foot" was printed in the 1952 *Best American Short Stories*, and "The Veldt" was printed in the 1960 *Britannica Library of Great American Writing* (Nolan 59, 63). Some of Bradbury's best-known stories are included in this col-lection, most of which are cautionary tale about the future, warning against the misuse of technology.

Fahrenheit 451 (1953), discussed in chapter 5, is one of Bradbury's two best-known and most influential works (the other being *The Martian Chronicles*). In this dystopian novel, Bradbury criticizes what he sees as major problems of American culture: the growth of a mass media that privileges the short-term and simplified cultural texts produced on tele-vision and the use of sterile technologies for education and transporta-tion, not to mention the Cold War potential for nuclear war.

Fahrenheit 451 shows the problems of American culture through the perspective of one man, Guy Montag, who is a fireman in a future world in which firemen burn books. As an adult, growing increasingly unhappy with his life, Montag is influenced by a young girl and an old man, a retired English professor, to question the world around him. Depressed and alienated, Montag at first tries to involve his wife and others in this process, but ends by killing a fire chief, burning his own house, and escaping from the city into the natural world that surrounds it. Just as Montag is leaving, the war planes that continuously fly overhead drop their bombs, destroying the city. The novel ends with Montag joining others who have memorized books and walking toward a future in which they hope to bring back books.

Dandelion Wine (1957), discussed in chapter 6, is the first of what Mogen characterizes as Bradbury's "autobiographical fantasies," fictions based on Bradbury's early life. These began appearing in the 1950s and have continued to appear through the 1990s. Although many of Bradbury's early stories contained images of the Midwestern town where he was born, *Dandelion Wine* is the first sustained exploration of that town and Bradbury's childhood experiences. Green Town, Bradbury's name for Waukegan, Illinois, is a fictionalized and poetic version of his hometown. In his introduction, Bradbury explains his method of writing through word association to revisit or recreate memories of his boyhood. His introduction supports Mogen's characterization of the works as containing fantastic elements as well as autobiographical ones, since Bradbury claims his intent was not to write a realistic novel but to recreate the sense of wonder, magic, and terror of his childhood. As with *The Martian Chronicles*, Bradbury selected and revised earlier short stories and added new chapters to create a unified work.

Dandelion Wine covers one summer in the life of twelve-year-old Douglas Spaulding (Ray Bradbury's middle name is Douglas), during which he comes to his first conscious realization that he is alive. With that realization, he also understands for the first time that he will die. While Douglas is at the heart of the novel, around him is Green Town—his family, friends, and even the terrifying Lonely One, a serial murderer. Friends leave and people die, and Douglas must come to terms with all aspects of life. Throughout the summer, he spends time writing all of his new ideas in a special book, showing, in a real sense, the birth of a writer who, decades later, is still writing to create as well as to understand the world around him.

Something Wicked This Way Comes (1962), discussed in chapter 7, is a novel often paired with *Dandelion Wine*, although the second novel is not exactly a sequel. Set in Green Town in the autumn, *Something Wicked* draws more on gothic and horror conventions to describe a different kind of coming of age experienced by the two young male protagonists, Will Halloway and Jim Nightshade. When a carnival comes to town, Will, Jim, and other townspeople are tempted by the dark seductions of the "Pandemonium Shadow Show." All the temptations involve the changing of time: younger characters are promised the benefits of growing up, perhaps including sexual maturity, while older characters are promised a return to the joys and nostalgic memories of their youth. A major element of this novel is the relationship between the two young protagonists; another is the relationship between a father and son, Charles and Will Halloway, who become closer through their efforts to defeat the dark carnival.

Death Is a Lonely Business (1985), discussed in chapter 8, is another of Bradbury's autobiographical fantasies, but this work is a mystery rather than a fantasy or horror novel. It is set in 1949 in Venice, California (where Bradbury and his wife first lived after they married). The narrator, whose name is never given, is a young writer trying to move from publishing short fantasy and weird tales to producing a novel. His fiancée, Peg, is spending several months in Mexico, and he is having a bad case of writer's block. All the stories the narrator mentions are Bradbury's own, although they are never mentioned by title, only plot. One late night coming home on a bus, the narrator encounters a man he first believes is a drunk. Later, when murders start occurring in the area, the narrator comes to believe that this man is in fact the murderer. He tells a police detective, Elmo Crumley, of his experiences and deductions, but Crumley is skeptical. But as the two continue to work together, the writer eventually solves the murder. The murderer's victims are all lonely, somewhat eccentric characters whom the writer knows, and the mystery plot is eventually overshadowed by the descriptions of settings, eccentric characters, and the books that both the narrator and Crumley are writing.

A Graveyard for Lunatics (1990), discussed in chapter 9, continues with the same narrator as *Death Is a Lonely Business*, set a few years later. Now married, the narrator is hired to work with his high school friend Roy Holdstrom (based on Bradbury's friend Ray Harryhausen) on a monster movie. This novel is set at a film studio in 1954 and opens on Halloween when the narrator, wandering by himself late at night, finds a note that directs him to the cemetery next door. There, at midnight, he sees a dead body that he recognizes as the former head of the studio.

Graveyard draws on the conventions of horror films, with a special homage to Lon Chaney's *Hunchback of Notre Dame*. Soon after the narrator's discovery of the body, strange events start to take place at the studio: shifts in assignments (the narrator is assigned to work on a religious picture), firings, cover-ups, and mysterious disappearances and deaths. The narrator calls on the help of his friends who appeared in *Death is a Lonely Business*, especially the police detective Elmo Crumley and Constance Rattigan, a retired film star. By a mixture of luck and persistence, the narrator eventually unravels the mystery, which has its roots in the studio head's "death" twenty years earlier. He also finishes the screenplay for the religious picture, which is possibly based on the 1961 film *King of Kings*, for which Bradbury wrote an uncredited narration for Orson Welles (Nolan 63).

Green Shadows, White Whale (1992), discussed in chapter 10, is the third of Bradbury's autobiographical works and is based on his life as a writer during the late 1940s and early 1950s. This novel focuses on the trip Bradbury made to Ireland to write the script for John Huston's film *Moby Dick*. Twelve of the thirty-two chapters were published independently as short stories. The fantastic elements in this novel are much reduced, usually to stories relating to the Irish, and a major portion of the novel is devoted to the relationship between the unnamed narrator, the director Huston, and Melville's white whale. The title of the novel plays on that of a book written about John Huston: Peter Viertel's *White Hunter, Black Heart*.

A number of the stories focus on the narrator's attempts to get to know the Irish, primarily in the persons of a group of men who spend time at Heeber Finn's pub and who tell "the Yank" stories about their lives and history. The other stories relate the narrator's volatile relationship with Huston, who began as one of his heroes but became "the Beast," dragging the unwilling writer through numerous physical and emotional adventures to prove his fortitude. The difficulty of translating Melville's huge novel into a screenplay compares with the difficulty of working with Huston's huge ego.

CONCLUSION

Bradbury published his first novel in 1947 and continues to write and publish. This chapter has only hinted at the volume and variety of his work published during the past fifty years, the extent to which his work remains in print and is still eagerly sought out by readers, and the pro-liferation of his work in various media including a computer game based on *The Martian Chronicles* and televised versions of his stories. The passion with which Bradbury approaches life as well as the way his writing embodies his life may be one reason for that popularity, which cannot be explained by any genre designation or marketing label. Whatever critical terms or categories are applied to Bradbury, it seems safe to say that he is regarded as one of the major American writers for his contri-butions to American literature.

3

The Martian Chronicles
(1950)

The Martian Chronicles (*TMC*) is possibly the best known and most critically acclaimed of Bradbury's work. First published in 1950, *TMC* has been continuously in print, in both America and Britain, ever since. *TMC* has been marketed as science fiction, but it more closely fits what some critics call science fantasy. As Joe Patrouch, a scholar of fantastic literature, argues in "Symbolic Settings in Science Fiction: H. G. Wells, Ray Bradbury, Harlan Ellison," Bradbury's Mars is "scientifically inaccurate by the science" of the 1940s; instead, it reflects the "rural, small-town Midwest of Bradbury's childhood" (Patrouch 41). Bradbury makes it clear in one of his introductions that he never intended to write a scientifically accurate version of the colonization of Mars because such a vision would go out of date in a few years. Despite the implausibility of his vision, Bradbury notes in his introduction to the 1997 Avon edition that he is still regularly invited to speak at the California Institute of Technology, which shows the enduring power of myth (xii). Further evidence of this mythic power is the recent adaptation of *TMC* as a computer game.

This chapter references the Avon "updated and revised" edition published in 1997. This edition includes an introduction by Bradbury describing how he came to write *TMC*, noting the early influence of Sherwood Anderson's *Winesburg, Ohio* and describing his visit to New York and his conversation with Walter Bradbury (no relation), the Doubleday editor who inspired him to think of a book incorporating his Martian stories. This edition is different than the first American edition in two ways.

The first and more substantial change is in the selection of stories: two have been added ("The Fire Balloons" and "The Wilderness") and one has been dropped ("Way in the Middle of the Air"). The second change is more subtle but also important: a revision in the dates included with the story titles in the table of contents and on the first page of each story. Critics do not include the dates when referring to the story titles, so this change is only apparent in the table of contents. The 1950 edition dates its first story as taking place January 1999, its last in October 2026; the cycle of stories thus covers a twenty-seven year period, beginning approximately fifty years after the first edition was published. In the 1997 edition, the first story is dated January 2030, the last one October 2057. The stories still cover a twenty-seven year span, and the first story is dated approximately forty years after the edition's publication date. Bradbury's chronology in both editions suggests a near future to contemporary readers.

Of the twenty-seven stories in the revised edition, sixteen of them are full stories, of varying lengths, with named characters. The eleven other pieces are the "bridge" sections, short passages with descriptions of events rather than individual characters, making transitions or setting up the stories, which focus more on characters in conflict.

PLOT DEVELOPMENT

The genesis of *TMC* lies in an editor's suggestion that Bradbury combine various previously published short stories set on Mars into a unified whole. As with the book's model, Sherwood Anderson's *Winesburg, Ohio*, critics have debated whether the text constitutes a true novel. Some, knowing that a number of the stories were published independently, consider the work more a collection of stories than a novel. However, Jonathan Eller's careful analysis of Bradbury's process of revising those earlier stories to create *TMC* supports the claim that this book is Bradbury's first novel.

In "The Body Eclectic: Sources of Ray Bradbury's *Martian Chronicles*," Eller, one of the scholars who has devoted the most time to studying Bradbury's work, considers all of Bradbury's Mars stories, a number of which were never considered for *TMC*, describes the various plans or lists Bradbury created at different stages in composing the book, and closely compares the earlier stories with Bradbury's revised versions that were included in *TMC*. Eller concludes that, "viewed as a process, the transformation of these tales helps to define the structural and thematic unities of the book, and to determine just what kind of book it is" (Eller 377). Eller argues that since "more than half of the composite text [of *TMC*] is new or rewritten," and the five different editions published in America and Britain over the years show no more than a "5% variation in content," Bradbury, in creating *TMC*, "essentially wrote an entirely new book" (Eller 401–2).

Eller's textual analysis and use of Bradbury's original composition materials show impressive scholarship. However, even readers who lack the training or access to such materials can see the structural unity of *TMC* in its text. Bradbury's title gives a hint of that unity. "Chronicles" are historical narratives, usually associated with the Middle Ages, in which events are described by people living at that time and are usually arranged chronologically under annual headings, focusing on a single place. For example, *The Plantaganet Chronicles* covers England in the High Middle Ages (circa 1000–1300), focusing on military, political, and religious events. Similarly, *The Martian Chronicles* offers not a random collection of stories about various characters but a unified narrative about the history of human colonization of Mars. That narrative unity is found in the "metaplot," the story line that connects the various stories, not just in the plots within the stories.

The first seven stories describe the start of exploration of Mars and the failure of the first three expeditions. This first section also establishes the probability of atomic war on Earth and the near-extinction of the Martians from chicken pox.

The next thirteen stories detail the settlement of Mars. First come small groups of men, who deal with loneliness ("The Settlers"), set up mining communities, and plant trees ("The Green Morning"). Then comes a mass migration; houses are built and communities established ("The Locusts" and "Night Meeting"). A second wave of settlers arrives from the urban areas of America (a brief explanation in "The Shore" suggests that other nations are too concerned with "thoughts of war" (119) to colonize Mars). Following the settlers come institutions. Priests build churches ("The Fire Balloons"). More buildings for settlers ("Interim") are constructed. Families appear, with children playing among the ruins ("The Musicians"). Women leave Earth to marry the men in the settlements ("The Wilderness"). Place-names are given, and regulatory agencies and rules follow ("The Naming of Names" and "Usher II"). Finally, the rich, the tourists, and the elderly move in as well ("The Old Ones" and "The Martian").

The next three stories detail the beginning of the atomic war on Earth (speculated about in "The Luggage Store" and witnessed in "The Off Season" and "The Watchers"), and the start of the evacuation whereby the rockets take the colonists back to Earth.

The next two stories relate what happens to people who missed the evacuation: "The Silent Towns" describes the "last man" on Mars (or so he believes). In "The Long Years," which takes place twenty years after the war and evacuation, Hathaway's death leaves Captain Wilder to discover that the marooned man's family members are robots.

The last two stories describe the destruction on Earth and the last human survivors. "And There Will Come Soft Rains" describes the final breakdown of an automated house on Earth, and "The Million-Year Picnic" ends the novel with the story of a family who has escaped the final destruction to settle on Mars.

CHARACTER DEVELOPMENT

Narrative Point of View

Most of the sixteen full stories are told in the third-person, limited omniscient point of view. This narrative perspective describes not only the actions and speech of all characters but can also report the feelings and thoughts of selected "point of view" characters. In *TMC*, the stories tend to have a single point of view character, focusing attention and empathy on that character and showing readers events through this individual's perceptions and beliefs.

The eleven bridge sections are written in third-person objective, or "fly on the wall," perspective, which places the narrative focus on exterior events, without reference to any characters's feelings or emotions. Through the use of these multiple narrative perspectives, Bradbury presents a complex and multi-layered view of humans colonizing Mars.

Martian and Human Characters

Individual sections present both Martian and human characters. The Martians are described as brown-skinned and golden-eyed, survivors of a declining civilization who try to defend themselves against the encroaching humans. The humans are presented, for the most part, as arrogant and invasive, unappreciative of the complex civilization of the Martians and interested only in appropriating the planet's mineral resources. A few humans are described as more sensitive and aware, dedicated to studying the dead or dying civilization around them.

The first individualized characters seen in *TMC* are called Martians, although the use of the term implies a point of view that is still human. Groups of characters are mentioned in "The Rocket Summer," but not in any detail. "Ylla," the second story, describes how a Martian couple's life is disrupted by dreams that the wife, Ylla, has of an alien. Ylla's telepathic contact is with an earthling, Nathaniel York, who is coming to Mars. Her husband, Yll, reacts with jealousy to her enthrallment. "The Summer Night," the third story and one of the bridge pieces, shows that what happens to Ylla was not an isolated incident. One summer evening in a community on Mars, everyone, adults and children, come into telepathic contact with earthlings, shown by their singing or reciting English poetry.

The first human characters arrive in "The Earth Men": a crew of four men (the Second Earth Expedition) arrive at Mrs. Ttt's house. The earthmen are comic and blustering, insisting that some major celebration be held in their honor and pouting when none of the Martians take them seriously. The Martians seem bored and unimpressed, sending the men on to others who will deal with them. The men finally realize that the Martians believe they are hallucinations, products of one insane Martian's mind. A Martian psychologist, Mr. Xxx, then shoots them all, and himself, "proving" they are hallucinations.

The rest of the stories all focus on human characters, mostly males. "The Taxpayer" is a bridge episode, focusing on a man who insists that he wants to leave Earth for Mars because of an impending atomic war. He is treated as insane, but his apprehensions are proved correct by the end of the book. "The Third Expedition" focuses on several characters out of a crew of seventeen: Captain John Black, Navigator Lustig, and Samuel Hinkston. This expedition lands on Mars only to find an exact reproduction of Captain Black's hometown, and all the crew's dead friends and family alive again. By the end of the story, all the humans are killed by Martians who have taken the form of their friends and families.

"—And the Moon Be Still as Bright" describes the Fourth Expedition, especially the conflict between Jeff Spender and the rest of the crew. They have arrived to find virtually all the Martians dead of chickenpox, carried by an earlier expedition. Spender's mourning for the death of an ancient civilization leads him to try to murder the rest of the crew. The characters in this story fight over the question of how settlement will occur, and Spender's death and Captain Wilder's departure leave Mars open to exploitative colonization. Several characters first introduced in this story reappear in later ones: Parkhill, Hathaway, and Captain Wilder.

The next three sections, "The Settlers," "The Green Morning," and "The Locusts," describe colonization without going into detail about any characters other than Benjamin Driscoll, who in "The Green Morning" goes out to plant trees to change the Martian atmosphere. "Night Meeting" describes the only meeting between a human and a Martian character that does not lead to the death of either. Tómas Gomez and an unnamed Martian meet each other in the middle of the night. This meeting is one out of time: each character believes his "present" is the real one and the other individual is a hallucination or vision of the past. Starting with misunderstanding and fear, they come to accept the necessity for inhabiting their present moment without trying to prove what the other one is. Neither the human or the Martian's perception of their meeting is privileged by the story. This poetic interlude, showing a meeting of minds between two characters who are able to put aside their fear of a being from an alien race and communicate with each other, is one of the most haunting stories in the book.

"The Shore" describes the kind of settlers who come to Mars in more detail, though not as individual characters. "The Fire Balloons" (not included in the 1950 edition) focuses on a group of Episcopal priests who are leaving Earth for Mars. They debate whether their main mission should be saving the sinful humans living in a frontier society or going to the remaining Martians to save their souls. Father Peregrine, the main character, wants to go to the Martians because he is fascinated with the idea of the existence of new kinds of sin, but Father Stone rejects that idea. By the end of the story, the fathers have made contact with the "Old Martians" (globes of blue fire, which appear only in this story), and both Father Peregrine and Father Stone have learned something new about each other and about the nature of spirituality and sin.

"Interim" and "The Musicians" describe the development of towns and the arrival of families. The settlers build towns just like Iowa, and adolescent boys regularly play a game that involves going to the ruined Martian cities and scuffing through the remains of the dead Martians like they were dead leaves.

"The Wilderness" (not included in the 1950 edition) is the only story to describe the experiences of Earth women in the colonization of Mars. This tale focuses on Janice Smith and Leonora Holmes on their last night on Earth as they finish their preparations to leave for Mars. Janice is going to marry Will, who has built a house for her just like her home. The two main characters are not the only women leaving; the story describes thousands getting ready to move out. These characters are the "good women," that is, virtuous women whose main goal is to become the wives of settlers. Brief references in earlier stories to "bad women" ("Fire Balloons" and "The Shore") mention the other kind of women, presumably prostitutes rather than wives. After listing the first settlers as "men accustomed to space. . . . the coyotes and cattlemen," a narrator says that "Everyone knew who the first women would be" (119). The Mayor in "The Fire Balloons" also complains about the "wicked women" who came in with the workers.

"The Naming of Names" further describes the process of settlement, with humans giving names to the Martian landscape and tourists coming in. "Usher II" contains a more fantastic character than the rest of the stories. Stendhal, a man obsessed with the greatness of Edgar Allan Poe and incensed against government censorship of literature, plans a revenge based on Poe's stories. Stendhal sees colonizing a new planet as a means of escaping a spreading government bureaucracy that burns books.

With the spreading settlement and the growth of bureaucracy come older settlers. "The Old Ones" describes the elderly coming to Mars, and "The Martian" describes a deadly contact with a Martian. An old couple find their long-dead son Tom one night, but when they go to town he cannot keep his shape. As the humans in "The Third Expedition" learned, Martians can take on or appear to take on the shapes of humans through their telepathic powers. The emotions of the humans in "The Old Ones" force the Martian through many shapes until he finally dies.

The final stories focus on characters more concerned with what is happening on Earth than on Mars. "The Luggage Store," a short bridge piece, relates a conversation between the owner and Father Peregrine about the ominous news from Earth. "The Off Season" focuses on Sam Parkhill, one of the crewmen from the Fourth Expedition and his hotdog stand. He's the final example of the "Ugly American" colonist: blustering and never contradicted by his wife, who obviously sees more than he does. Planning to earn a great living from his hotdog stand, he learns that atomic war has broken out on Earth. This story reveals that some

Martians did survive the disease and have been hiding out in the hills; they are the ones who bring the news to Sam. "The Watchers" describe all the colonists coming out to see the war on Earth, the fire of the bombs exploding, and their decision to return to Earth.

"The Silent Towns" is a comic view of the aftermath of the exodus from Mars: Walter Gripp, a miner, misses the evacuation. Enjoying the luxury goods left behind, he discovers there's at least one woman left on Mars. Enthralled by romantic visions of her beauty, he meets her only to discover that she's fat and ugly, which sends him racing off to be on his own again. "The Long Years" is a tragic vision of life on Mars after the evacuation. Mr. Hathaway (like Parkhill, a member of the Fourth Expedition) and his family miss the evacuation because of their archae-ological research. Twenty years later, Captain Wilder returns from his own twenty-year mission to Jupiter and searches for anyone left on Mars. Hathaway signals the rocket, but dies before he can leave Mars. Wilder realizes that Hathaway's family members are not humans, but robots built to replace the wife and children who died. Wilder leaves the robots on Mars and plans to go to Earth to see what has happened but as "There Will Come Soft Rains" reveals, there is little human life left on Earth either, just an automated house running down.

The final story, "The Million-Year Picnic," describes an American fam-ily, a husband and wife and three young sons, who escaped from war on Earth to resettle Mars. They plan to meet with another family, with daughters, to begin another colonization effort. The book closes with the image of the family looking at themselves in the water of one of the canals and seeing the Martians.

SETTING

Most of the stories in *TMC* are set on Mars, with a few exceptions. The first story, "Rocket Summer," is set in Ohio when the first rocket to Mars is launched. The fifth story, "The Taxpayer," returns to that lo-cation as Mr. Pritchard yells through the fence surrounding the Third Expedition's rocket that he wants to go to Mars, fearing an atomic war and other ills of Earth. Both "The Fire Balloons" and "The Wilderness" (added to the revised edition) and "Way in the Middle of the Air" (re-moved from the revised edition) begin on Earth, but describe groups leaving to colonize Mars (specifically, the Episcopal Fathers; women en-gaged to, or hoping to marry, men on Mars; and African Americans in the South). Otherwise, no stories are set on Earth until the twenty-sixth (next to last), which describes what happens to an electronically controlled house after the atomic war. With the exception of this last story, each story with an Earth setting shows characters who want to go to Mars.

THEMES

Some humorous episodes mitigate the overall serious tone of the novel. The Second Expedition's travails and Walter Gripp's ill-fated meeting with the last woman on Mars are both comic. The gothic grotesqueries of "Usher II" are a comic homage to Edgar Allan Poe, showing a character taking glee in murdering "censors" by methods taken from Poe's stories. However, the major theme of *TMC* is a commentary on the negative effect of American civilization's reliance on certain kinds of technologies. This novel's perspective on technology is why some science fiction writers and critics say that Bradbury represents a minority view in the science fiction tradition, especially in the context of science fiction of the 1950s, which tended to celebrate the importance of technology in improving life for humanity.

A more somber tone pervades the earliest stories describing the Martians as a dying race who are mostly destroyed by a human disease, as well as the depiction of humans as arrogant and uncaring about the history and culture of the planet's original inhabitants. The destruction of Earth by atomic war and the final image of one family being the last, or nearly the last, humans alive complete the elegiac, or funereal, tone of the novel.

Two critics have created different interpretations of *TMC*. In "*The Martian Chronicles* and *Fahrenheit 451*: Ray Bradbury's Cold War Novels," critic Kevin Hoskinson analyzes *TMC* as Bradbury's major statement about the Cold War, the conflict between the United States and the Soviet Union that grew after the end of World War II. *TMC* especially focuses on the fear of atomic bombs destroying the world. Linked with that sense of precariousness, Hoskinson notes, is a conflict between individuals and society, especially the conflict between those who conform to a majority culture and the individuals who do not fit in. Bradbury's ongoing interest in the power of technology to suppress individual freedom and identities as well as spirituality and art can also be seen in the book.

Gary K. Wolfe, in "The Frontier Myth in Ray Bradbury," presents a different reading of the novel. Wolfe argues that Bradbury reflects the same sense of the frontier myth that Frederick Jackson Turner made at the 1893 Chicago world's fair. Turner's presentation, titled "The Significance of the Frontier in American History," argued that the presence of the frontier was the major shaper of American history and culture. Wolfe analyzes the extent to which *TMC* expresses on Turner's ideas, without claiming that Bradbury studied Turner. Turner's basic idea is a familiar element in science fiction; Wolfe notes that the phrase used in the television and film series *Star Trek*, "Space—the final frontier," shows how a popularized version of Turner's historical argument exists even in contemporary televised science fiction.

ALTERNATIVE PERSPECTIVE: A POSTCOLONIAL READING

Postcolonialism is a theory of literary analysis that was developed in the 1980s to focus on literature written in English by writers from cultures once colonized by Great Britain or the United States. Such literature has been written for some time, although the term and analytical approach are recent. The major focus of postcolonial analysis is what happens when "one culture is dominated by another. As postcolonial critics . . . point out, to be colonized is to be removed from history. In its interaction with the conquering culture, the colonized or indigenous culture is forced to go underground or to be obliterated" (Bressler 266).

While postcolonial analysis tends to focus on the literatures of formerly colonized cultures, a growing number of scholarly works apply postcolonial methods to science fiction to explore the extent to which cultural struggles between different human cultures are represented in the symbolic guise of "aliens" and "humans."

TMC shows a struggle between two cultures with specific historical parallels. The chicken pox that destroys the Martians recalls the diseases that destroyed many of the indigenous cultures of the Americas. Current research suggests that in the first four centuries after European contact, perhaps 90 percent of the indigenous peoples in the Americas died, with diseases and warfare being the two primary causes (Hirschfelder 36–38). Bradbury's descriptions of the "waves" of settlers and frontier imagery indicate he wished to evoke the settlement of North America. "The Wilderness" (not in the 1950 edition) makes an overt parallel between the 1849 California gold rush and the Martian colonization.

Bradbury's novel does not celebrate the glories of the colonization of Mars. His sympathetic portrayal of Martian characters (one of whom tells the expedition that the real name of the planet is Tyrr), along with the few human characters who are dedicated to the peaceful study of Martian civilization are two ways the novel questions the process of colonization. Characters who are scholars or intellectuals (Spender, who quotes poetry and studies the language and art; Hathaway, who is an archeologist) or who are from cultures other than Anglo or European American (Tómas, who encounters a Martian) are presented in more detail and with more sympathy than characters who brag about the colonizing of Mars.

"Way in the Middle of the Air," which appeared only in the 1950 edition, also presents the point of view of a culture rarely represented in science fiction of the 1940s and 1950s. This story describes the emigration of African Americans from the southern United States to Mars. The narrative point of view is that of white Southern males, who view this exodus with repressed fear and hatred. Their feelings are expressed by one of them who attempts to stop a young man from leaving because of a debt. The white man's attempt fails when other African-American characters combine their resources to collect the amount still owed.

Bradbury's novel cannot be considered as expressing a completely postcolonial point of view, a thoroughly critical view of a colonizing power, but a postcolonial reading can focus on several key elements that undercut the simplistic glorification of American power in the 1950s. Some of this critical stance may well come from Bradbury's experiences as an artist in a masculinized culture in which art, scholarship, study, and imagination are perceived as effeminate. Postcolonial scholars argue that the men in a colonized culture are socially constructed as less than masculine/less powerful, thus occupying the same symbolic space as women do. Such men are figured as effeminate—as artists/intellectuals were during Bradbury's youth. He portrays male characters who wish to study the Martian culture and language as a minority within the colonization project, which is dominated by blustering men with little regard for culture.

The Illustrated Man
(1951)

The Illustrated Man (TIM) was first published in 1951 and has remained in print since that time. TIM consists of eighteen short stories presented within a framing narrative, a story split between the book's epilogue and prologue. A short story, "The Illustrated Man," was published in Esquire in 1950, but that story differs greatly from TIM's framing narrative. (Eller "Finding List" 36). Sixteen of the eighteen stories were published in various periodicals between 1947 and 1950, but two of the eighteen make their first appearance in print in the collection.

This book is widely considered one of Bradbury's strongest works. Three of the stories and the framing story were dramatized in a 1969 movie directed by Jack Smight: "The Veldt," "The Long Rain," and "The Last Night of the World." Bradbury was not consulted about the project, and critics do not consider the film as a total success.

Bradbury's decision to collect previously published stories and revise and arrange them have resulted in "novels" such as The Martian Chronicles, The Illustrated Man, Dandelion Wine, and Green Shadows, White Whale. The resulting texts are structurally and thematically unified.

Since Bradbury's regular collections of short stories have sold well and continue to do so, he must, as a writer, perceive a different purpose in revising and arranging stories to create a work such as TIM. Readers may find analyzing the work difficult because it lacks a single protagonist, unified settings, or an extended plot. However, a close reading of the conclusions and themes of the various stories reveals a unified narrative connection.

PLOT DEVELOPMENT

In the framing narrative, an unnamed first-person narrator is on a walking tour in Wisconsin and describes a meeting with an "Illustrated Man" (no names are given). When the Illustrated Man takes off his shirt, the narrator sees tattoos, or illustrations, that cover his body, and the man tells him how each illustration tells a story.

The Illustrated Man claims that his stories predict the future. One spot on the Illustrated Man's skin remains bare, but that spot will fill (temporarily) with information about the future of any person the man spends time with. The Illustrated Man warns the narrator not to look at the pictures, but he speaks as if he knows his warning will go unheeded. The narrator does watch the pictures, and sees eighteen tales enacted for him during the course of the night.

As arranged in the book, the eighteen tales are: "The Veldt," "Kaleidoscope," "The Other Foot," "The Highway," "The Man," "The Long Rain," "The Rocket Man," "The Fire Balloons," "The Last Night of the World," "The Exiles," "No Particular Night or Morning," "The Fox and the Forest," "The Visitor," "The Concrete Mixer," "Marionettes, Inc.," "The City," "Zero Hour," and "The Rocket."

The final section of the book describes what the narrator does when the stories stop: an image forms on the bare patch of the Illustrated Man's back, an image of the Illustrated Man choking the narrator to death. The narrator leaves, running down a road in the dark toward a small town that he knows he can reach before morning.

Bradbury's framing story serves to unify the narrative in two ways. First, the narrator experiences the stories in a single night and in a single location. Second, the Illustrated Man, a man too strange even for carnivals, links *TIM* to Bradbury's gothic stories, a carnival universe often suffused with horror. In an interview, Bradbury contrasted his childhood fear of carnivals with his early love for magic and circuses: "Carnivals are a combination. . . . not always evil, but dangerous. And you sense carny people are not nice people. They get out of town just after they've done something dreadful. . . . Only when you're older do you get some of the sexual overtones of carnivals" (Mogen 125). In *Something Wicked This Way Comes*, Bradbury presents the fully developed view of the carnival as embodying an evil, dangerous, but seductive universe. His associations of carnivals with horror and death are clearly made in the framing story of *TIM*, and the individual stories can be read against those background associations.

A second element that unifies these stories is that they all present specific views of the future. The narrator, by the end, believes that the stories predict the future, as shown by his decision to run away when he sees the image of his murder. Since he is able to escape to a nearby town, his survival reveals that the predicted future can be averted by the right action: the future revealed by the stories is not inevitable. Since he has survived to tell us the tales he saw that night, readers know the Illustrated Man did not later track him down and kill him. So the stories are perhaps less predictions than warnings of what might come and what might be averted.

What view of the future is revealed to the narrator? Above all, it will be worse than the present, rather than better. *TIM* does not endorse the idea of progress or the notion that technology will create a better future. Of the eighteen stories, only two, "The Other Foot" and "The Rocket," present a positive view of the future, and even these stories hardly qualify as optimistic. In the first, a third world war destroys Earth and only a few escape to the colonies on Mars, which have been settled completely by African Americans. In the second, the happy ending is gained by what amounts to a kind of virtual reality space ride, rather than actual travel to the stars. In the futures of *TIM*, technological progress does not solve humanity's problems. At least six of the stories involve the end of the world by atomic bombs or some other human means.

CHARACTER DEVELOPMENT

Seventeen of the eighteen stories are told in the third-person point of view, and each story focuses on a different protagonist, or main character. In a third-person narrative, one character is usually the main point of view character. Short stories do not allow as much development of character as do longer narratives, and more character development occurs through dialogue and description of actions than through in-depth descriptions of characters' thoughts and emotions. Stories also tend to focus on conflict between the main character and other characters.

In most of the stories in *The Illustrated Man*, the conflict between characters is described as the different perspectives between two groups of characters, rather than through a close focus on one or two individuals as is the case in three of the stories. In those three stories, the main character or characters embody a different perspective on events. "The Highway" focuses on Hernando, a Mexican peasant who earns a marginal living by farming and by scavenging the castoffs of the well-off tourists he watches drive north. On this particular day, his green and life-filled field is the setting for the news of an atomic war. The fleeing tourists insist that the end of the world has come, but through Hernando, readers see growth and life outside the cities of North America, which are destroyed.

Another story with a close focus on individual characters is "No Particular Night or Morning." This story focuses on Hitchcock and Clemens, part of a crew on a rocket far from Earth. The names of the characters evoke Alfred Hitchcock, the famous film director, and Samuel Clemens (Mark Twain). The central conflict of the story is between the two men's different perspectives on their situation, and the story is structured around a series of debates between them. Hitchcock is rapidly descending into an extreme solipsism, a condition in which he refuses to believe in the existence of anything outside himself, including Earth or other members of the crew. Clemens and the others try to intervene, but Hitchcock eventually kills himself by exiting the ship—in a spacesuit, however, which seems to show he has some sense of the material reality of space. Clemens is left alone, thinking of Hitchcock alone in space.

"The Fox and the Forest" describes a couple dealing with the end of their world. In this story, Roger Kristen and his wife, traveling under the assumed names of William and Susan Travis, try to escape from their time, a future in which all resources are devoted to an immense and destructive war effort. Their future has the technology for time travel, but restricts its use to vacations. The couple remain in 1938 Mexico, and kill a Searcher who came after them, but they are tricked by a group of American actors who are also Searchers, and are taken back to the future to help fight the war.

The characters in five stories are family members: children and parents in "The Veldt," "The Rocket Man," "The Last Night of the World," "Zero Hour," and "The Rocket," and married couples in "Marionettes, Inc." "The Veldt" presents an extremely negative view of the effect of technology on a family. George and Lydia Hadley have tried to give their children, Wendy and Peter, the best of everything, including a holographic nursery that is part of a completely automated house. George becomes nervous and tries to restrict the time the children are spending in the nursery. The children, whose names evoke James Barrie's Never-Never Land, have begun eliciting violent and destructive programming instead of the pleasant childhood fantasies their parents expected of them. The conflict leads the children to set up their parents to be eaten by the nursery's lions.

The families in the other stories also have problems associated with technology. In "The Rocket Man," a father absent because of his job in space is eventually killed in an accident, leaving his wife and son alone. "The Last Night of the World" describes a family representative of all the families on Earth. The adults have realized, through a universal dream message, that the world is coming to an end, and they quietly accept it, going about their daily business and then going to bed without telling their children anything. "Zero Hour" focuses on one family, Mrs. Morris, her daughter Mink, and her friends. During the course of an afternoon, Mink tells her mother all about "Invasion," a new game, but the mother does not take it seriously. Only at the end does she realize that the invasion is real and that the children have been participating happily, setting up the conditions which allow an actual force of unnamed and never fully described aliens to invade Earth.

"Marionettes, Inc." focuses on Braling and Smith, married men spending a night out together. They begin discussing problems in their marriages, but Braling has a solution: a marionette that is exactly like him. He plans to use the marionette to take a vacation in Rio without his wife's knowledge. Smith plans to get a marionette as well, but when he returns home and looks at his bankbook, he discovers ten thousand dollars (the price of a marionette) is gone and that his "wife" is ticking. Braling, returning home, finds himself completely replaced by the marionette Braling, who has fallen in love with Mrs. Braling and plans to take her to Rio after shoving the human Braling into a storage box.

Only "The Rocket" offers a family who love and are happy with each other. The father, Fiorelle Bodoni, is a junkman who takes a discarded rocket model and creates a virtual tour of the solar system. He takes his children on a wondrous tour, and is left at the end, promising to take his wife on her own trip a little later.

Four stories focus on characters who face conflicts between people from different cultures. In "The Other Foot," Bradbury describes a Mars that differs from his other Mars stories: in this story, African Americans left Earth in the 1960s and colonized Mars. The main point of view character in this story is Hattie Johnson, who left Earth in 1965 as a small girl. Some twenty years later, a grown woman married to Willie Johnson and a mother, she sees the arrival of a rocket bringing a white man from Earth. As in *The Martian Chronicles*, an atomic war has left millions of people dead, especially in cities. The survivors, about half a million, have sent the man to plead with the colonists for rescue. The first impulse of some of the African-American characters is to impose a racially based segregation, Jim Crow in reverse, on the white survivors. Hattie asks the man whether the place where Willie's father was lynched remains, and he shows her evidence that the town and its inhabitants were destroyed; only then does the mood change. The story ends with Willie proclaiming that everyone is equal, now that the majority of Earth's population has been destroyed.

Martian and human cultures conflict in "The Concrete Mixer," a story told from the point of view of a Martian, Ettil, who is part of an invasion of Earth. Ettil is reluctant to go; he has read so much of Earth's science fiction about failed Martian invasions that he is sure that humans have a sense of inevitable victory. Ettil's perceptions are critical both of his own people, who forced him to join the Legion of War, and of the Earth men and women who welcome them to Earth and then wear the Martian invaders down between the grindstones of feminine attention and the mass media. Since Ettil is the point of view character, readers share his thoughts and feelings about the other characters.

"The City" relates another conflict between an alien race and humans. Left by a dead race who was wiped out by the distant ancestors of humans, the city is the only remnant of this species, and is programmed to recognize and destroy the enemy and then die.

The same sense of inevitable doom, carried out by technology, surfaces in the conflict between literary and mythic characters and visiting humans in "The Exiles." In this story, Mars has become a refuge for fantastic characters from literature and myth and for the writers of such stories. The story's point of view moves back and forth between the literary and mythic characters and the human men approaching the planet in a rocket. Writers from Shakespeare to Poe and mythic characters such as Santa Claus have fled from the rational society on Earth, where most of their books and stories have been destroyed, to live on Mars. When a rocket arrives from Earth, the characters and authors try to destroy the men on the ship, but fail. After landing, the captain burns the last copies of the books he has brought from Earth, symbolizing their commitment to "science and progress" (104). The burning of the last copies finally destroys the apparently immortal creators and creations of literature and legend.

Five of the stories focus on groups of men who serve together in an organization or institution. The priests in "The Fire Balloons" (also printed in *The Martian Chronicles*) disagree on the nature of their mission and what sort of sin they will find on Mars. The conflict between Father Peregrine and Father Stone, the two major characters, is resolved when they become acquainted with the blue globes of fire who are the "Old Martians." Since the Old Ones have given up physical life, sins, specifically sins of the body, cannot occur.

"The Visitor" describes what happens to a group of quarantined men on Mars. Exiled because of a disease called "blood rust," they lead limited lives. When a man named Leonard Mark, who has the ability to create visions that seem real to all human senses, arrives in camp, the men quarrel over who should have his "services." Saul, the protagonist, does not want to share Mark with the other men, and in the ensuing fight they kill Mark.

The characters in "Kaleidoscope" are doomed at the beginning of the story because their rocket has blown up. Although they are in their space suits, they have no chance of rescue. All they can do is talk to each other by means of the radios in their suits for a limited time. The story focuses on Hollis, the main point of view character, who realizes he is headed toward Earth. All the characters move through fear, helplessness, and anger. The Captain tries to restore order by giving commands, but the men no longer accept his authority. Hollis's coming to terms with the quality of his life and what it means to die is paralleled by the other men starting to see more beauty around them. Hollis's final realization is of the beauty of the universe, the individuality of each person's journey, and the hope that he can make up for his past life. At the end of the story, the point of view shifts to a small boy in Illinois seeing a "falling star" that the reader knows is Hollis's body entering the atmosphere.

Another kind of death, spiritual death, is explored in "The Man," a story in which an expedition from Earth lands on an inhabited planet only to find that its arrival is of little interest to the inhabitants. When the crew is told that a "remarkable man," described in ways that evoke Jesus Christ, had just appeared in the city, the Earth men quarrel over whether the appearance of this man is a hoax, a hallucination, or a genuine Visitation. Captain Hart becomes obsessed with travelling on to other worlds and catching up with the man, but Martin, and most of the crew, stay behind because they realize they have found what they sought.

"The Long Rain" tells the story of a military unit on Venus searching for shelter. They are engaged in a war with an enemy that is never clearly described or named. The men, mostly referred to by rank instead of name, must find a Sun Dome for shelter from the unending rain. Only the lieutenant survives to find a working dome, and in the end he could be merely hallucinating the shelter.

Besides the framing story, only one story is told in a first-person narrative and contains more of a psychological description and development of the narrator and protagonist: the seventh story, "The Rocket Man." The narrator in this story is a boy named Doug whose father is a Rocket Man, gone from Earth for three months at a time. Doug lives with his mother leading a life that seems to revolve around the short times his father returns, but he plans to go to space like his father. The narrator's name recalls Douglas Spaulding in *Dandelion Wine* (and Douglas is Bradbury's own middle name). The family lives in Green Village, a variation of Green Town, Bradbury's fictionalized hometown of Waukegan, Illinois. The son tells what it is like waiting for his father to return and the glory of his father's job. When his father dies, pulled into the Sun, Doug's mother responds by shutting out daylight and the Sun—and pulls her son as well into a life where they try very hard never to see the Sun.

The central characters in most of the stories are humans. In the one exception, "The Concrete Mixer," the point of view character is a Martian named Ettil, who is reluctantly persuaded to join an invasion of Earth. The story presents a humorous take on the "Mars Invasion" when the humans first surrender, then overwhelm the invading army with adulation, feminine attention, and the media. Bradbury's alien character allows him to give an outsider's view of American capitalist media culture. In this darkly comic story, the Martian invasion fails because America welcomes the invaders and essentially swallows them. Ettil writes home about the horrors of the American automobiles and cinema that eventually kill him, foretelling the destruction of the invading army.

SETTINGS

While the eighteen collected stories in *TIM* vary greatly in terms of characters (no character appears in more than one story) and time period, Bradbury does create a sense of unity through his settings, which are related to his themes. George Slusser argues in *The Bradbury Chronicles* that the period from 1946 to 1955 was one of intense creative activity for

Bradbury. During this time, he was exploring three "thematic land-scapes": "outer space, future dystopia, and what can be called 'the odd corners,' " the third category being stories about human eccentricity (26).

The stories in *The Illustrated Man* can be described in terms of these three categories. Eleven of the stories are set in space itself or on Mars or other planets. Ten stories are set completely, or in part, on Earth. "Kaleidoscope," "The Rocket Man," and "No Particular Night or Morning" are set completely in space, or focused on space, and all three stories relate the death of one or more characters. Five stories are set on Mars. One of the five, "The Fire Balloons," has been published in some later editions of *The Martian Chronicles*, but the other ones are what Eller calls "unchronicled" Martian tales: stories set on Mars that are not included in *The Martian Chronicles* and which sometimes contradict that book's account of Mars. The five stories set on Mars are "The Fire Balloons," "The Exiles," "The Visitor," "The Concrete Mixer," and "The Other Foot." This last presents a very different version of the colonization of Mars than that in *The Martian Chronicles*: in this story, only African Americans have settled on Mars, having left earth in 1965. After an atomic war destroys most life on Earth, the survivors send a ship to beg the colonists for help.

"The Visitor" is set in a quarantine camp on Mars, where men suffering from a disease called "blood rust" are exiled. "The Exiles" is set on a Mars that has served as a refuge for the authors and characters of literature and myth to save themselves from the modern age (2120) on Earth, where their books have been banned and burned. "The Concrete Mixer," like "The Other Foot," presents a different perspective on Mars because the story is told from the perspective of a Martian, Ettil, part of an invading army.

Three stories take place on other planets: "The Man," set on an unnamed planet visited by an American spaceship; "The Long Rain," set on Venus; and "The City," set on an unnamed planet visited by an American spaceship. In "The Man," a rocket from Earth arrives at a planet where a major spiritual event has just occurred, and conflict arises when the human crew debates how they should react to it. "The Long Rain" is set on Venus during a human war with an unnamed opponent. "The City" suggests that humanity did not evolve on Earth, but settled it 20,000 years ago after fighting a war. The titular city has been left by a dying race to exact revenge against an enemy that used biological weapons—the ancestors of humans.

Of the eight stories set on other planets, six focus on death and de-

struction, including the deaths of individual men, Martians, literary characters, and the world population. Of those eight stories, only one has
any sense of human survival: when the African Americans living on
Mars reject the temptation to impose segregation and racial oppression
on the white survivors of a third world war. Two of the stories, those
dealing with specifically spiritual themes, do present an optimistic view
of the future: the Episcopal priests in "The Fire Balloons" gain a new
sense of God, and the crew in "The Man" give up a doomed mission to
travel to every possible world to stay behind, sharing the spiritual insights gained by the natives of the planet where a Christ figure has just
appeared.

Ten of the stories are set completely, or in part, on Earth, most in a
future in which humanity misuses its technology: "The Veldt," "The
Highway," "The Rocket Man," "The Fire Balloons," "The Last Night of
the World," "The Fox and the Forest," "The Concrete Mixer," "Marionettes, Inc.," "Zero Hour," and "The Rocket."

"The Veldt" describes how the misuse of technology turns two children into killers. "The Highway" is a short, ironic story of a Mexican
farmer's view of "the end of the world." "The Last Night of the World"
is another story about the world coming to an end, not by means of a
bomb (though bombs exist), but through a mysterious outside agency,
never identified, that sends a dream to all adults. "The Fox and the Forest" shows two time travelers who are fleeing horrendous conditions in
their present, decried by one character as "a great black ship pulling
away from the shore of sanity and civilization, roaring its black horn in
the night, taking two billion people with it . . . to death . . . into radioac-
tive flame and madness" (116). Ultimately, the couple are caught and
returned to this future.

"Marionettes, Inc." is a story about robots that are marketed as human
substitutes but which manage to take over the lives of the human buyers.
"Zero Hour" describes how a children's game turns out to be the first
move in an invasion by hostile forces that have recruited the children to
act against their parents. The last story before the "Epilogue" is "The
Rocket," a story about how a poor junk man, dreaming of the wonders
of space, creates a virtual tour for his family, one of the book's few trips
to space that does not end in death.

Bradbury's vision of future technology and its use within families or
by national governments warns his readers of its negative potential. Only
the final story shows an apparently more positive view of the use of

technology to explore space, although the fact that eighty years of space travel have not changed things for Fiorello Bodoni and Bramante places the joy of space exploration firmly within a social and economic context. For these men, whose families still "live in shacks like our ancestors before us," and whose children may not be able to achieve their dreams of going into space (178), real space travel remains inaccessible.

THEMES

Thematically, *The Illustrated Man* is a warning to readers against certain futures that Bradbury saw as possible during the early 1950s. The narrative frame encourages readers to look at the stories as warnings about futures that can be changed or avoided. Calvin Miller, in "Ray Bradbury: Hope in a Doubtful Age," argues that the character of the Illustrated Man, wearing the stories on his flesh, can be read as a "tangible metaphor" for Bradbury himself, or any storyteller (Miller 94).

Thus, the plots and themes of the selected stories are unified in Bradbury's intention to warn his readers against too great a dependence on technology, against too great a reliance on governments or capitalism, and against rejecting our past myths and supernatural literature for a sterile and unimaginative modernity. Visions of possible futures are presented for the purpose of trying to avert those futures.

From children programming a hologram nursery, to atom bombs destroying the Earth, to a complex city programmed by a dying race to take revenge no matter how many millennia pass, technology in *TIM* is used to cause destruction and death. Even the Sun Domes, a technology to create an Earth environment on Venus, serve a military purpose. Nonmilitary technology (automobiles and media technology) are also presented negatively. The use of technology to travel into space is presented as destructive. Rocket ships explode, or carry the worst aspects of American culture to other planets. With the exception of two stories, "The Other Foot" and "The Visitor," the interactions between Americans and aliens are violent and coercive. Only Fiorello Bondi's imaginary spaceship, one of illusion, is presented in a positive way.

Space colonization shows that the worst aspects of American culture can be transported to other planets or can overwhelm even an invading alien force: an African-American colony, twenty years removed from Earth, has to deal with the history of racism and oppression that the adults experienced on Earth. Human colonization of Mars mirrors the Anglo-European conquest of the American West: "It's a frontier now, like in the old days on Earth, out West, and in Alaska" (78).

Life on Earth in these views of the future is no more positive: over half the stories involve the deaths of major characters or complete world destruction. Children and parents are alienated from each other, and spouses want to escape from their marriages. And, according to the time travellers of "The Fox and the Forest," things are likely to continue getting worse.

ALTERNATIVE PERSPECTIVE: "RACE" AS A LITERARY CONSTRUCT IN SCIENCE FICTION

Until recently, science fiction has been a field that many readers thought of as being written primarily for, and by, white men. A similar assumption is that race could not be a major focus of this literature, and thus not an area for analysis. Newer critical theories have brought questions of gender and ethnicity to the discussion of science fiction. Earlier writers, readers, and critics of science fiction, fantasy, and horror have been mostly Anglo-American, or "white." Critical perception and public memory of the earlier decades of science fiction, especially those decades referred to as a genre's golden age (the 1940s and perhaps the 1950s), is of "whiteness." Until recently, "whiteness" was considered the normal situation, not needing to be marked by any specific terminology. Author Toni Morrison argues that the concept of "whiteness" depends on "blackness" to define it, that whiteness can only be understood in terms of its "opposite" in America.

In *Playing in the Dark: Whiteness and the Literary Imagination*, Morrison encourages critics to reexamine earlier texts and analyze their interlocking constructions of "whiteness" and "blackness." A later anthology, *Criticism and the Color Line: Desegregating American Literary Studies*, takes on the challenge by analyzing authors such as Mark Twain, Frederick Douglass, Fanny Fern, Anna Julia Cooper, Harriet Beecher Stowe, and other major literary figures, as well as slave narratives. As important as this anthology is, it neglects the marginalized literature of science fiction. However, questions about how "whiteness" and "blackness" define the American literary landscape are applicable to popular and genre fiction as well as to the more elite literatures.

The Illustrated Man appeared in 1951. While critics have noted that the book can be analyzed in the historical context of McCarthyism and the Cold War, a review of what was happening in the Civil Rights movement of this time can provide another kind of historical context that is not always considered in relation to science fiction because of the presumption of "whiteness" being the norm. The focus on the history of whites (Anglo-Europeans) and the major military/political conflicts of this period can be modified by a brief review of some of the important (but often invisible because not taught) civil rights events of the period. Some important events noted in *Timelines of African American History: 500 Years of Black Achievement* in 1950–51 are as follows:

> Four thousand delegates attended the National Emergency Civil Rights Conference in Washington, D.C.;
>
> The National Association for the Advancement of Colored People (NAACP) filed suit to integrate elementary and secondary schools in districts in Kansas, South Carolina, Virginia, and Washington, D.C., eventually leading to the 1954 Supreme Court decision *Brown v. Board of Education of Topeka*;
>
> The Supreme Court ruled against segregation in dining cars on trains (*Henderson v. United States*), and ordered law schools in Texas, Virginia, and Louisiana to admit African-American students;
>
> For the first time, an African American won the Nobel Peace Prize (Ralph Bunche, for his work in Palestine);
>
> For the first time, an African American won a Pulitzer Prize for literature (Gwendolyn Brooks, for *Annie Allen*);
>
> African Americans in general continued a long-standing tradition of fighting for equal rights and access in such diverse areas as politics, religion, education, literacy, the military, and sports. (Cowan 215–19)

Morrison argues that one useful strategy for breaking down the national and literary assumptions that African Americans were not present (invisible) in politics, culture, and literature is studying the "Africanist" presence in American literature. By this she does not mean African Americans. Instead, Morrison uses the term to mean "the denotative and connotative blackness that African peoples have come to signify, as well as the entire range of views, assumptions, readings, and misreadings that accompany Eurocentric learning about these people" (Morrison 7). The

assumptions that Morrison challenges are those made by literary scholars, not by the actual writers of literature. These scholars, Morrison
charges, ignore the presence of African-American characters in the works
of white (canonical) writers as completely as they ignore the works of
African-American writers.

Three of Bradbury's stories include African Americans (using the term
"blacks") as major characters: "The Big Black and White Game" (from
The Golden Apples of the Sun), "Way in the Middle of the Air" (in earlier
editions of *The Martian Chronicles*), and "The Other Foot" (from *The Illustrated Man*). Although the first two stories are told from the perspectives of white male characters, "The Other Foot" is told from the point
of view of an African-American couple, Hattie and Willie Johnson.

The Johnsons are two of the original colonists on Mars in a future
where the only colonists are "Negro" (the word used in the story). The
only characters in the story are white and black, specifically American
characters. Most of the people on Earth have died in a third world war;
the (white) messenger in the rocket says, "I don't think there are more
than five hundred thousand people left in the world, all kinds and types"
(35). The survivors have built one rocket to come ask the colonists to use
their original rockets to return to Earth and rescue the survivors.

The first response of the men is to recreate Jim Crow segregation—
separate water fountains, schools, housing—and to threaten the recreation of lynching. Women, and the children born since colonization, react differently, but it is only the messenger's assurance that the towns and
cities where the adults suffered oppression are completely destroyed that
makes Willie and the other men rethink their original impulse. While the
positive ending to the story may be considered overly idealistic by some
readers, Bradbury's creation of a future Mars settled entirely by African
Americans is an image of "blackness," of an Africanist presence in the future, that is striking for the time in which he wrote the story.

Wayne Johnson may be the only critic to acknowledge Bradbury's stories dealing with minorities to any extent. In a chapter discussing Bradbury's treatment of "Mexico, Ireland, Homosexuals . . . Blacks, China,"
Johnson notes that "The Other Foot" is a role-reversal story common in
science fiction (Johnson 133). Johnson praises the realistic story published
in 1945, "The Big Black and White Game," in which a twelve-year-old
white boy watches a baseball game between white hotel guests and the
black servants. "Way in the Middle of the Air," set in the South in 2003
before the events of "The Other Foot," describes whites watching all the
town's blacks leaving for a rocket to Mars. Johnson notes that the stories

are dated, since the social and political changes taking place in 1950 make it unlikely that Jim Crow segregation could survive for another fifty years, until 2003. However, he notes the extent to which Bradbury's stories are still unusual for science fiction (or other literature) of the time.

Questioning the way race and power are associated in American literature brings attention to other outsiders in Bradbury's work: Ettil, the Martian character who comes reluctantly to Earth; the children who, as Lahna Diskin argues in "Bradbury on Children," are presented as a separate race, hostile and antagonistic to their parents in "The Veldt" and "Zero Hour" (Diskin 152). These stories all present views of how minority populations or less powerful individuals experience possible futures described by Bradbury.

Fahrenheit 451
(1953)

Fahrenheit 451—the title refers to the temperature at which paper burns—has its origin in Bradbury's earlier novella "The Fireman," published in *Galaxy* in February 1951 (Eller "Finding List" 37). In a 1982 afterword, Bradbury describes how he wrote the original novella in a basement typing room at the library of the University of California at Los Angeles, where he could type for half an hour for a dime. He finished the novella in nine days. When he took breaks, he would walk through the stacks, enjoying the feel and smell of the books. The importance of libraries, places maintained by governments that contain books accessible to all, is at the heart of this novel.

The original novella was expanded (roughly doubled) into a novel, *Fahrenheit 451*, published in 1953. Francoise Truffaut adapted the novel for a 1966 film that Bradbury believes to be the best of the many film adaptations of his work (Johnson *Ray Bradbury* 139), and Bradbury himself adapted the story for the Studio Theatre playhouse.

Fahrenheit 451 is considered one of Bradbury's best works. Like *The Martian Chronicles*, it received praise from mainstream critics seldom accorded those works published and marketed as "science fiction" during the 1950s. The novel has been in print continuously, and has received a great deal of critical attention from academics.

Rafeeq McGiveron has published two academic essays on *Fahrenheit 451*: "What 'Carried the Trick': Mass Exploitation and the Decline of

Thought in Ray Bradbury's *Fahrenheit 451*" discusses the issue of what caused the decline in society; readers and Bradbury himself tend to blame pressure from minority groups within society for the decline, but the text itself shows more of the blame belonging to mass culture. McGiveron's " 'Do You Know the Legend of Hercules and Antaeus': The Wilderness in Ray Bradbury's *Fahrenheit 451*" analyzes the importance of the wilderness in the novel as both beautiful and optimistic but also humbling and powerful. Another scholar, Kevin Hoskinson in "*The Martian Chronicles* and *Fahrenheit 451*: Ray Bradbury's Cold War Novels" shows how both novels deal with social issues America faced during the Cold War years, especially "government oppression of the individual, the hazards of an atomic age, recivilization of society, and the divided nature of the 'Cold War Man' " (Hoskinson 346).

Susan Spencer, an academic critic who writes on literacy issues in science fiction, compares *Fahrenheit 451* with another dystopian novel, *A Canticle for Leibowitz* (1960) by Walter M. Miller, in a discussion of the way the two novels present the "post-apocalyptic library," the existence of an oral tradition, in which knowledge is handed down verbally, and a literate tradition, in which knowledge is written down. Diane Wood, in "Bradbury and Atwood: Exile as Rational Decision," compares *Fahrenheit 451* to Margaret Atwood's novel *The Handmaid's Tale* (1985) in their strongly political visions of a future mass culture in which reading is a heroic act. Mogen devotes a chapter to the novel, focusing on its satire of McCarthyism and its lyrical intensity.

PLOT DEVELOPMENT

Fahrenheit 451 is organized into three titled sections: "The Hearth and the Salamander," "The Sieve and the Sand," and "Burning Bright." The novel chronicles the protagonist's, Guy Montag's, change from acceptance of and pleasure in his job as a fireman, through his questioning of history and society, to his final rebellion against his job and country.

"The Hearth and the Salamander" describes events that begin Montag's transformation. The first event is his encounter with Clarisse McClellan, a seventeen-year-old neighbor who meets him late one night as he comes home after his shift. She asks him several questions, specifically what firemen used to do and whether he is happy. Montag tries to laugh off these questions, but the conversation reminds him of a meeting he had a year before with an unnamed old man, whom he later comes to know as Faber. When he enters his house and goes into the bedroom he shares with his wife, he finds she has attempted suicide. While the emergency team he calls pumps her stomach and replaces her blood, he thinks about her other suicide attempts. The third event is when the firemen are called to burn a collection of books owned by an old woman who chooses to burn with her books rather than leave.

The fourth event is Clarisse's death; she is killed in a hit-and-run accident, a common event that is not investigated as a crime. As a result, Montag feels ill and does not want to return to work. Chief Beatty comes to talk to Montag, giving him information about firemen, the official story of how their job evolved, and how important the firemen are in protecting society. Montag is not convinced. He shows Mildred the books he has been hiding for a year, ever since his first conversation with Faber in the park.

In the second section, "The Sieve and the Sand," Montag tries to explain his new ideas to the people around him. He first tries to talk with Mildred about the possibility of war, but she invites her friends over to watch the telvisor, a combination virtual-reality room and television, reminiscent of the nursery in "The Veldt." Montag then goes to Faber, whose address he had from their first talk, with one of the books he rescued, the Bible. Faber gives Montag a different sense of history than Beatty's version. He tells Montag that there are three things missing from Montag's—and everyone's—life: the quality information or details that exists in good books, leisure time, and "the right to carry out actions based on what we learn from the interaction of the first two" (85). What has taken the place of these things is the superficial information put out on the telvisor and "off-hours," which Faber insists are not the same as leisure.

Faber and Montag try to work out some means of resisting the firemen, or some other way of bringing back the forbidden books. Faber is afraid, but Montag forces him to agree to help by threatening to destroy the Bible. Faber knows a printer and agrees to work with Montag to set up an underground press. When Montag leaves, he has a radio through which Faber can talk to him.

Instead of pursuing the plan to set up a press, Montag returns home and tries to convince Mildred and her friends to question their views and read books. He reads them Matthew Arnold's poem "Dover Beach," but all three women respond angrily. Mildred tries to make up a cover story about how the firemen are allowed to bring one book home to share with their families as long as they incinerate it afterwards, and

Montag does incinerate the book. Montag leaves the women and goes to the firehouse to confront Captain Beatty and the other firemen. While he's arguing with the captain, a call comes in, and they all go. When they arrive at the address, it's Montag's house, and he learns the call was made by Mildred.

The third section, "Burning Bright," describes Beatty giving Montag the choice of burning his own house and the books. The Mechanical Hound is present to enforce the burning. Montag does burn his house, but also burns Beatty and the Hound. Montag finds four books Mildred had missed, then escapes. He takes the books and hides them in one of firemen's house and calls in an alarm, then goes to Faber's house. Faber tells him that war has been declared, and they watch a televised chase by another Mechanical Hound. They decide to try to cover Montag's scent, and Faber decides to leave the city for St. Louis. After a long chase, Montag makes it to the river and floats to freedom.

As he makes his way through a wilderness that surrounds the city, he meets a group of men who have formed an underground movement to remember books. They help him by giving him a potion to change his body chemistry, or scent, and show him how the televised hunt for him resulted in an innocent man's death. As they are talking the next day, they hear jets overhead and hear bombs destroying the city. At the end, the men are walking north, planning to wait out the war and then start a movement to write and make their books available.

CHARACTER DEVELOPMENT

Guy Montag is the novel's protagonist and its main point of view character. He is the only character whose thoughts and emotions are described for the reader (other than a couple of short sections that report the Mechanical Hound's point of view). Since the major focus of the book is Montag's transformation from a dedicated fireman to a participant in an underground library movement, the use of the third-person perspective allows the reader to follow Montag's development, witnessing how he responds to the events and characters around him.

The opening section is a scene from Montag's point of view. This section does not use Montag's name and is primarily composed in the passive voice, a sentence structure that denies that any subject has agency, or the power to act. The first line of the novel is "It was a pleasure to burn" (3). The lack of a name and the passive voice constructs Montag as representative of all firemen, anonymous, focused on the pleasure inherent in the process of destroying books, houses, and people.

Montag begins to question his life and society and comes to the realization that neither he nor his wife Mildred are happy. His unhappiness is shown by his hiding of forbidden books, and her unhappiness surfaces in regular attempts to commit suicide. Montag begins to wonder why he is unhappy. By the end of the novel, Montag has become an active participant who has claimed his own agency; leading a group of men through the wilderness, he recites part of what he has memorized from the Bible. Planning to share his "book" with his fellow "librarians," Montag begins to take on the status of a leader, someone who is planning a better future.

The other characters in the novel serve as either catalysts or supporters for Montag or as antagonists who work against him, and are described in terms of the effect they have on him. The characters Clarisse and Faber contribute most to his change and support him, while Mildred and Captain Beatty oppose his attempts to change and become his antagonists.

The same characters interact with Montag throughout the novel. He is influenced by Clarisse's disappearance, Mildred's addiction to the "TV parlor," or televisor, and Faber's own attempts to resist the socially driven destruction of all books, as well as people who try to save books. Pressure from the Fire Chief and Captain Beatty and the ongoing announcements of war that punctuate the novel also contribute to Montag's change.

Montag's prominence as the protagonist results in a greater narrative focus on his development as a character than is the case for the other characters. What he thinks about his marriage and wife Mildred, his sense that they have both lost something (which Mildred denies when he tries to talk to her about it), his fear of the Mechanical Hound, his attraction to Clarisse, as well as his childhood memories and perceptions of the men he works with all create a characterization with emotional depth. Other characters' actions and speech are described, but no information on their thoughts or feelings is given.

The reasons why other characters do what they do is not as clear, but their effect on Montag is described. Clarisse and Faber have important conversations with Montag that cause him to doubt his social function and way of life. Clarisse, a young woman who lives with her family near Montag, likes to do things most people consider crazy: walk at night; talk about happiness, love, and nature; and question what is presented as normal or socially appropriate. The other character who supports

Montag in his changing ideas is Faber, a retired English professor, who has been trying to work out a solution to the book burnings on his own. He has not moved to active resistance because, as he tells Montag, he's a coward. One of the main functions Faber serves in the novel is to answer some of Montag's questions and to give him ideas for how to change what he is doing. Faber shelters Montag from the Mechanical Hound and helps him escape to the countryside, where he meets an underground resistance movement, consisting of mostly philosophy and literature professors who are remembering books that they hope to write down after the war.

Two characters in the novel serve as antagonists and represent the larger antagonist in the novel, American society: Mildred and Captain Beatty. Mildred, Montag's wife, is addicted to the televised mass culture provided nonstop; she sees the characters in her programs as more real than her husband. However, her unacknowledged unhappiness with her life is shown by regular suicide attempts. After Clarisse's disappearance, Montag challenges Mildred. After one conversation, Montag brings out books he's been hiding for a year, since his first conversation with Faber. Mildred's first response is to try to cover up for him in some way, then to withdraw even further into her TV parlor; eventually, she turns him in. Mildred does not want to question society's reliance on technology and its choice to burn books. She does not remember her suicide attempts and denies that she is unhappy in any way.

Captain Beatty is a more active antagonist. Beatty represents the institutional or government voice, while Mildred is constructed as a consumer of the TV parlor's representation of the world. Beatty presents the official history of the firemen to Montag, but Beatty is also able to quote a great number of books and to recognize the source of something Montag had read. Beatty can quote Philip Sidney, Alexander Pope, Dr. Johnson, and a plethora of other authors not identified in the text (105–6) as he argues against Montag's desire to save and read books. The Fire Chief quotes books to prove that the texts contradict each other. His knowledge of books along with his position show that the government allows some people in power access to books as long as they remain dedicated to burning books owned by individuals. Chief Beatty finally pushes Montag to his limit, and Montag kills him.

SETTING

Fahrenheit 451 is set in an unnamed city in the United States, possibly in the Midwest, in some undated future. The sole geographical references are the fact that the city has a bus station where Faber can take a bus to St. Louis and Montag's memory of meeting his wife in Chicago. The only time referent is Montag's comment that the country has started two atomic wars since 1990. Within the city, certain locations are specified as important: Montag's house, which is in the suburbs, Faber's house, and the fire station where he works a night shift. At the end of the novel, Montag has escaped the city by means of a river and is traveling through a countryside, or wilderness, with other men, all of whom have memorized books and plan to write them down after the war has ended.

THEMES

Fahrenheit 451's major themes of resistance against the conformity imposed by a mass media and the use of technology to control individuals are linked to its depiction of a dystopia. As M. Keith Booker explains in *Dystopian Literature: A Theory and Research Guide*, one strategy dystopian literature takes is to criticize existing social and political systems by extending the premises of those systems to reveal their flaws (Booker 3). Much of the science fiction published in the 1940s and 1950s presented technology as a positive force and space travel as a happy prospect for humanity; at the same time, America was engaging in World War II, which led to the development of atomic bombs and to the Cold War. Both Hoskinson and Mogen have examined the extent to which *Fahrenheit 451* criticizes McCarthyism and Cold War attitudes. The novel also criticizes American attitudes toward and dependence on technology.

Bradbury's main theme is the extent to which technology can be used for social control, specifically through the use of the mass media for all education and entertainment. The novel describes people being bombarded twenty-four hours a day by "TV class," "film teacher[s]," and TV parlors and televisors. The technology is used to promote a mass culture and to suppress individualism. American reliance on the automobile is also singled out as a major problem, with Clarisse being killed in a hit-and-run accident, Mildred driving fast in the country and killing animals when she is depressed, and Montag himself nearly being killed by a group of teenagers in a car.

The dystopian future in the novel is also created by the social control of history and knowledge, enforced through the technology of book burning. Since access to printed knowledge and books is restricted, the only source for information is the government, which presents a distorted and simplified view of history. The government is not the only cause of this future: Beatty and Faber claim that the American population, in its desire for positive images and simplicity, demanded the suppression of books as complex, contradictory, and difficult. Beatty tends to blame "minority groups" such as specific religions, ethnic minorities, professional groups—anyone who objected to depictions in books. Faber insists that the "public itself stopped reading of its own accord. [The] firemen provide a circus now and then at which buildings are set off and crowds gather for the pretty blaze, but it's a small sideshow indeed and hardly necessary to keep things in line" (87).

While some dystopias (such as George Orwell's *1984* [1949]) put all the responsibility for oppression on the government, Bradbury's novel does not show the national government acting in any way, with the exception of periodic references to planes flying overhead with bombs. Only after most Americans chose to give up reading, seduced by the simplicity and presence of the mass media, did the government step in. As McGiveron argues in "What 'Carried the Trick,' " Bradbury's novel is more an indictment of mass culture than of a specific system of government.

ALTERNATIVE PERSPECTIVE: A STYLISTIC READING

One way of analyzing a literary work is called stylistic analysis. This sort of analysis looks closely at how a writer chooses and arranges words. A stylistic analysis can focus on the author's choice of words, grammar, or syntax (sentence structure). Usually a stylistic analysis will focus on one kind of stylistic choice (such as images) or, if on a variety of choices, on a fairly short excerpt from the work. Stylistic analysis always considers how the style contributes to the work's theme or the overall meaning.

Images are words that evoke sensory impressions: touch, taste, smell, sight, hearing. Images provide a sense of the physical reality a character experiences in a story. In realistic fiction, images are not necessarily foregrounded, that is, given a great deal of attention. Such images often serve more as background information, meant to be taken literally for their descriptive value. But in other genres, images take on the importance they have in poetry: that is, they sometimes act as symbols, with abstract or thematic meanings as well as a literal or descriptive meaning. The term "image cluster" is used when a writer builds in a number of references to a core image.

Bradbury uses images associated with fire and burning as well as images of light and running water, throughout *Fahrenheit 451*. The novel's reliance on a specific pattern of images is discussed in detail by Donald Watt in " 'Fahrenheit 451' as Symbolic Dystopia." Watt provides a careful description and analysis of how these images are associated with important characters and events throughout the novel. Images used to describe events or characters make the novel a "symbolic dystopia" for Watt, with the stylistic choices Bradbury makes resulting in a subtle and distinctive dystopian novel. Watt shows how Bradbury's use of fire imagery, with fire as both negative and positive, sets up two symbolic poles (196).

A stylistic reading can show how Bradbury brings together his three major image clusters in a short passage near the end of the novel. At this point in the story, Montag has escaped a Mechanical Hound by going into the river. Floating downstream, he is thinking about his life and the choices he has made. He previously planned to take violent action against the firemen, and has killed Captain Beatty. But after this passage, he decides not to destroy or burn anything else. Instead, he will try to preserve knowledge and life:

> He saw the moon low in the sky now. The moon there, and the light of the moon caused by what? By the sun of course. And what lights the sun? Its own fire. And the sun goes on, day after day, burning and burning. The sun and time. The sun and time and burning. Burning. The river bobbled him along gently. Burning. The sun and every clock on the earth. It all came together and became a single thing in his mind. After a long time of floating on the land and a short time of floating in the river he knew why he must never burn again in his life. (140–41)

This passage has 112 words, arranged in thirteen sentences, although six of those sentences are fragments (lacking either a subject or a verb). Little action takes place: Montag is floating, passively, in the river. He sees and, by the end, he knows. The river is what moves him ("bobbled him along gently"). Since the passage lacks action verbs or, in some sentences, any verbs, the nouns attract greater attention: there are twenty-eight noun phrases, including verbals, the -ing forms of verbs, which can function as nouns or modify nouns. (There are also two verbs, "lights" and "burns" which closely parallel similar nouns.) One-quarter of the words in this passage, then, are in noun phrases.

The nouns are mostly related to Bradbury's image clusters: *sun* is used six times; *fire* and *light* are each used once. The verbal *burning* is used five times. *Moon* is used three times, and closely associated with the sun (its light comes from the sun), and *sky* is used once. *River* is used twice, and *land* and *the earth* once. The contrasting images of burning (of fires and of the sun) are brought together with the water of the river and the land. The moon, "low in the sky," is nearly touching the land, and it connects the light of the sun with the earth and water. "It all" becomes "a single thing" to Montag. The other major image cluster is related to time: *time* occurs four times, *day* twice, and *clock* once. The passing of time is paralleled with the sun in two sentences: "The sun and time. The sun and time and burning."

The images in this passage have all been used before, throughout the novel, to describe characters and events, and Montag's perceptions of them. This view of the universe, in which the opposing or destructive forces meld with the nurturing or creative forces, is a vision that results in Montag's decision to move away from destruction, even destruction for a "good cause," and toward preservation. Described in a deceptively simple style, these perceptions lead him to a new consciousness and a final decision on how he should live his life from this point on. After he leaves the river, he shortly joins the underground resistance group and commits to joining their project of memory and preservation.

Dandelion Wine
(1957)

Dandelion Wine (*DW*) is one of Bradbury's autobiographical fantasies, a novel that fully embodies Bradbury's love for creating eccentric characters and exploring their lives. The novel is more autobiographical than fantasy (unlike its companion, *Something Wicked This Way Comes*), with the majority of events being daily moments of life in the Midwest in the late 1920s. The main character, Douglas Spaulding, is based on Bradbury. In an introduction written in 1974 Bradbury describes how this novel originated with a writing method that used word association to access memories of childhood.

Considered one of Bradbury's strongest works, the novel has received a good deal of acclaim and critical attention. John B. Rosenman compares *DW* to Faulkner's short story "That Evening Sun" in its use of symbolic settings that represent heaven and hell. In "The Fiction of Ray Bradbury: Universal Themes in Midwestern Settings," Thomas P. Linkfield examines three novels set in the Midwest: *Dandelion Wine, Something Wicked This Way Comes,* and *The Halloween Tree,* arguing that Bradbury's themes—fear of death, nostalgia, and the necessity of accepting reality—are universal or literary, rather than particular to science fiction.

Loren Logsdon, in "Ray Bradbury's 'The Kilimanjaro Device,': The Need to Correct the Errors of Time," identifies the central idea in Bradbury's fiction as the need to correct "serious mistakes in time." While Logsdon's main focus is the short story identified in the title, he notes that both *DW* and *Something Wicked This Way Comes* depict characters who focus too much on either their pasts or their futures, ignoring the present moment to their detriment.

This novel is often compared with *Something Wicked This Way Comes*. Both are set in Green Town, and both have protagonists clearly based on Bradbury himself. Both novels share a concern for the passage of time and the maturation of young men. However, important differences also exist between the novels. *Something Wicked* (discussed in chapter 7) has a more clearly developed plot structure focusing on conflicts between characters. *DW* is set in the summer, *Something Wicked* in the autumn. Events in *DW* are not clearly organized in a linear plot. The unifying structure of the narrative is chronological (summer 1928), but the pace is more leisurely and apparently realistic: that is, the narrative focuses on events that take place during that summer, but the underlying pattern is not clear on a first reading.

PLOT DEVELOPMENT

The novel is structured in forty titled but unnumbered sections, ranging in length from one to seventeen pages. Events on the first three days of summer are described in detail in the first eleven sections: The story opens with Doug bringing summer into being at dawn. That same day, Doug and Tom go into the woods to pick grapes and strawberries with their father, and pick the first batch of dandelions for their grandfather's dandelion wine. Later, Doug runs with his friends Charlie and John to the Ravine and realizes he needs new tennis shoes. That same night, he sees the perfect pair in Mr. Sanderson's store window. On the second day of summer, Doug goes to Mr. Sanderson's store to buy the shoes (called "Royal Crown Cream-sponge Para Litefoot"); since he's short one dollar, he persuades Mr. Sanderson to try on a pair of the shoes to understand why he needs them so badly. He also offers to run errands for Mr. Sanderson, who agrees.

Later, Doug tells Tom about his plan to write about this summer, keeping a list of the rituals that are the same and another of those that change. On the third day of summer, Doug helps his grandfather bring out and set up the porch swing. That evening, all the families come out to sit on their porches as well, and the conversations are an image of eternity; Doug lies on his porch, listening to "these voices, which would speak on through eternity, flow in a stream of murmurings over his body. . . .

Sitting on the summer-night porch was so good, so easy and so reassuring that it could never be done away with. These were the rituals that were right and lasting. . . . the voices chanted, drifted . . . while the moths, like late appleblossoms come alive, tapped faintly about the far street lights, and the voices moved on into the coming year. . . ." (31–32).

The first eleven sections set up major elements of the novel: Doug's relationship with his family, his newfound realization of being alive, his friendship with John Huff and Charlie Woodman, his new tennis shoes, his writing, and his strong connection to his home town. Other important events are described as well: the conversation outside the cigar store that leads Leo Auffman to try to build a happiness machine, which eventually burns up, and his realization that his family is the true happiness machine.

Other events relate to chores around the house: the semiannual rug beating and cleaning, Bill Forrester trying to plant a new grass lawn that won't need mowing. Doug's grandfather is able to talk him out of this attempt. Later events move out more into the town. Tom has encounters on his own, with Mrs. Bentley and Elmira Brown, but he always mentions them to Doug, who then adds the insights: Mrs. Bentley teaches them that "Old People never WERE children" (79). Elmira Brown's accusation that Clara Goodwater is a witch leads Doug to think about witches and what powers they might have. Doug goes with Charlie and John to hear Colonel Freeleigh's stories, and the boys realize that the hundred-year-old man is a time machine. Doug also goes on the last ride of the trolley, before the new buses come in.

More serious events start taking place during the second half of the novel: in the 21st section, John Huff tells Doug that he's leaving town because of his father's job. Colonel Freeleigh dies of a heart attack, and Doug finds his body in the 25th section. Miss Lavinia Nebbs kills a tramp—or, perhaps, the Lonely One—in the 30th section. Finally, Doug's great-grandmother takes to her bed and dies in the 32nd section. Doug's response to that, as written, is that he cannot "DEPEND ON *THINGS* BECAUSE" machines die or don't work, and even tennis shoes fail to fly, and he cannot "DEPEND ON *PEOPLE* BECAUSE . . . *they go away . . . strangers die . . . people you know fairly well die . . . friends die . . . people* murder *people . . . your own folks can die*," leading him to the realization that he can die, although he does not write the word down (186–87).

His realization of his own mortality leads Doug to try to rescue Mr. Black's Tarot Witch, a wax fortune teller at the arcade. Deciding that she is a real fortune teller in need of rescuing from villains, Doug and Tom steal the Tarot Witch one night after Mr. Black, drunk, breaks the glass case that holds her. But Black catches the two boys near the Ravine and hurls the Witch over. Doug retrieves her, and his father helps them set her up in the garage. Doug's plan is to rescue her, free her from what he decides was an evil spell that imprisoned her in the form of the tarot witch, and have her tell his fortune so that he can avoid all dangers and live forever.

Soon after, Doug is stricken with a kind of heat prostration. The doctor cannot help, and only Mr. Jonas, the junkman, bringing two bottles of cool air for Doug, helps revive him. Tom tells Mr. Jonas about the bad events of the summer that he believes made Doug want to give up living. After Doug decides to live, he returns Mr. Jonas's favor by saving the family and the boarders from Aunt Rose's meddling with Doug's grandmother's cooking. When the grandmother is left alone in her messy kitchen with her bent spectacles, she turns out meals of ambrosia. When Aunt Rose cleans and organizes the kitchen and furnishes the grandmother with new glasses and a cookbook, the resulting food is terrible. Aunt Rose is sent away, but Grandma cannot return to her former culinary brilliance until Doug disarranges her kitchen, burns the cookbook, and hides the new spectacles.

Summer's end is now at hand—the first sign being school supplies in the dimestore window. The boys and their grandfather share one last conversation as they bottle the last batch of dandelion wine. The boys remember the summer, day by day, in great detail. Their grandfather remembers only the attempt to plant grass that doesn't need cutting. Doug brings the summer of 1928 to an end that evening.

The events of the summer are strung like beads, connected by the thread of conversations as the characters take time to talk about what the events mean. The first event singled out for conversation is Doug's decision to write about the things that happen that summer. Tom agrees to contribute to the list, so their conversations often lead to new entries on the list. Other important conversations take place on the front porch; everyone participates in these, and they occur throughout the summer.

In the sections immediately after certain events are described, Doug and Tom talk about the event. Singled out for discussion are Mrs. Bentley's age, Colonel Freeleigh's stories being a time machine, John Huff's leaving, Elmira Brown's accusation of Clara Goodwater being a witch, Colonel Freeleigh's death, Bill Forrester's relationship with Miss Helen Loomis and the lack of happy endings, Miss Lavinia Nebbs killing the tramp, Doug's plan for the Tarot Witch, and, finally, the heat that eventually strikes Doug down.

Important sections are indicated through another structuring device, one that is easy to overlook: punctuation. At the end of eleven sections, the final punctuation is an ellipsis (three dots), rather than a period. A period, as a mark of punctuation, means a full stop, a complete thought. An ellipsis, on the other hand, gives the effect of a thought that is incomplete or ongoing. The placement of ellipses at the end of eleven sections, primarily when Doug is thinking about what just happened (which is how the majority of sections end), draws attention to Doug's thoughts as an ongoing process.

CHARACTER DEVELOPMENT

Main Characters

The main characters are Douglas Spaulding, aged twelve, and his extended family (father, mother, brother Tom, grandparents, and great grandmother); Doug's best friends (John Huff and Charlie Woodman); the boarders, especially Bill Forrester; and assorted townspeople. The townspeople are businessmen, neighbors, and friends of the family: Mr. Sanderson sells Doug his new pair of tennis shoes; Leo Auffman, the town jeweler, is asked by Doug to make a Happiness Machine. Two extremely old characters, Mrs. Bentley (ninety-five), and Colonel Freeleigh (one hundred), have important relationships with Doug, Tom, and the other children. Doug is fond of riding with Miss Fern and Miss Roberta in their Green Machine, an electric car. Elmira Brown, wife of the postman, involves Tom when she accuses Clara Goodwater of being a witch. Miss Lavinia Nebbs returns from the movies one night to confront and kill the man who might be the Lonely One, what would now be called a serial killer, who has been killing women. Mr. Jonas, the town junkman, saves Doug when he nearly dies of heat and sadness.

A number of the townspeople change because of events in the novel, and these changes parallel Doug's experiences. The other characters deal with the problems of how to achieve happiness in life, how to deal with age and change, and how to face death. Doug also faces these problems throughout the novel. At the beginning of the novel, he becomes aware, conscious, of being alive. Later, because of the events of the summer, including his best friend's leaving town and his great grandmother's death, Doug also comes to the conscious realization that someday he will die. This crisis of existence is the sign of Doug's maturity, his movement into adulthood, his awareness of perfect life slipping away.

Doug details this change by writing about it. As he explains to Tom, showing him a pad of paper and a brand new Ticonderoga pencil, Doug has set up two lists: the first one is titled "RITES AND CEREMONIES," the second one "DISCOVERIES AND REVELATIONS," or maybe "IL-LUMINATIONS" or "INTUITIONS" (27). The first list is for what they do every summer, the rituals. The second list is for new events, in part, new ideas about what they do all the time. An example of the new things is Doug's "finding out maybe that Grandpa or Dad don't know everything in the world" (26). In fact, Doug's "power" to create and shut down summer 1928, described at the beginning and end of the novel, is not really magic. This power is the power a writer has, a profound doubling emphasizing that Douglas Spaulding is a character based on Ray Bradbury not only in the details of his life, but in his role as writer.

Two other characters are important to the novel, although they are not described in detail: The Lonely One, who has killed three women, and more abstractly, Death, the real antagonist in the novel. The Lonely One is perceived by the characters as a monster. When Miss Lavinia Nebbs kills an intruder in her house, Doug, Tom, and Charlie are quite sure that the short, bald, fat man is not The Lonely One, who in their imaginations is a tall, pale, and skinny figure who still haunts the Ravine. In the abstract, both Tom and Doug fear death, but Tom, despite one episode of fear when he and his mother go to the Ravine to find Doug, has not really accepted the possibility of his own death as Doug has.

Narrative Point of View

DW's narrative point of view is third-person, limited omniscient. This narrative perspective can describe the actions, dialogue, thoughts, and emotions of any of the characters, but usually focuses on one major point of view character, often (but not always) the protagonist. In Dandelion Wine, the major point of view character is Douglas Spaulding, a twelve-year-old boy and the protagonist of the novel.

However, other characters become point of view characters in certain sections. Several family members, one of the boarders, and a number of townspeople carry the point of view in one or more sections: Doug's brother Tom (two), Doug's grandfather (one), and great grandmother (one); the boarder Bill Forrester (one); and townspeople Leo Auffmann (three), Mrs. Bentley (one), Miss Fern and Miss Roberta (one), Elmira Brown (one), Colonel Freeleigh (one), Miss Lavinia Nebbs (one), and Mr. Jonas (one). These characters are minor in terms of narrative time, but they provide a deeper understanding of events related to the novel's theme.

SETTING

The setting is Green Town, Bradbury's fictional version of his home town, Waukegan, Illinois, during the summer of 1928—about a year before the 1929 stock market crash that heralded the Great Depression. Certain locations within the town are important: Doug's grandparents' house, which is also a boarding house, the Ravine, front porches, and the countryside in which the boys run wild during the summer. The novel opens and ends with Doug in the cupola of his grandparents' house, where he sleeps at times and from where is able to overlook the town. Through his gestures, he symbolically brings summer into being and then ends it.

THEMES

The major theme of *Dandelion Wine* is the development of a kind of self-consciousness of being alive, an awareness that is connected to the awareness of one's mortality. Bradbury assigns the timing of this revelation to the shift from childhood to adolescence. As Marvin E. Mengeling points out in "Ray Bradbury's *Dandelion Wine*: Themes, Sources, and Style," this novel is part of an American tradition of initiation stories in which a young protagonist matures through "rites of passage" involving self-discovery (Mengeling 878).

Doug's rite of passage begins in a moment of self-knowledge or self-realization (epiphany) at the beginning of the book, when he discovers that he is alive. This consciousness of living is soon followed by a series of events that teach him that an important part of being consciously alive is realizing that one will die. Through leavetakings and deaths around him, Doug comes to an understand of his mortality. This knowledge is difficult. At one point, worn down by the events of a hard summer, he nearly decides to die, but Mr. Jonas helps him "decide to live," and Doug then rejoins the community both mature and committed to passing on Mr. Jonas's good deed. This he does when he helps his grandmother regain her way of cooking for the boarders.

Another theme related to time is memory, expressed through the metaphor of dandelion wine, which Doug's grandfather makes at specific times throughout the novel. Bradbury discusses the importance of the metaphor in his introduction. The events that became sections of the book were pressed out of his memory like the wine is pressed from the dandelions. Three pressings, at the beginning, middle, and the end of the novel, echo the three months of summer. The care with which the wine is made is shown by the careful and lengthy description of combining of dandelions, picked by the boys, with clean rain water collected in a barrel. The resulting wine is then bottled in cleaned ketchup bottles, one numbered bottle for each day of the summer. During the third harvest and pressing that ends the book, their grandfather tells Doug and Tom how dandelion wine is the best way to save the summer: "Better than putting things in the attic you never use again. This way, you get to live the summer over for a minute or two here or there along the way through the winter, and when the bottles are empty the summer's gone for good and no regrets and no sentimental trash lying about for you to stumble over forty years from now" (236).

Dandelion wine becomes a symbol of time in the novel: a way of counting the days of summer, of storing memories to last through the years (but not in an acquisitive or overly sentimental fashion), and a strong sensory image that embodies the process by which Bradbury created the novel.

ALTERNATIVE PERSPECTIVE: A GENDER READING

Gender criticism is an approach to literary analysis that builds on the earlier work of feminist critics and draws on later work by gay and lesbian critics and by scholars in the newly developing field of men's studies. The basic assumption of gender studies is that while some aspects of maleness and femaleness may be biologically determined, social gender roles—masculinity and femininity—are learned and reflect specific cultural beliefs and specific social or historical contexts (Bressler 270).

Bringing the ideas of gender analysis to Bradbury's *Dandelion Wine* complicates any idea that this novel describes a universal theme of initiation or maturation and leads the reader to question how the novel presents the issues of what it means to be a preadolescent boy in a Midwestern town in the 1920s.

The family in *Dandelion Wine* is an extended family: several generations live, if not in the same house, close to each other. Doug, his brother Tom, and his father and mother live together, but close by is the boarding house where Doug's great-grandmother, grandmother, and grandfather live with various boarders. Other family members apparently live close by.

From the start, the novel makes clear that its central journey is one toward masculine maturity: Doug and Tom go with their father into the woods. This male journey into the woods, or wilderness, is a traditional theme in American literature. The woods, or the wilderness, around "civilization" are a domain inhabited by wild or untamed animals. The Ravine in the novel is another kind of wilderness, a more threatening place that only the "older boys" go to. Doug's mother is not a part of this journey, nor is she described as knowing what results. Later, Doug and his male friends Charlie and John run through the Ravine, while Tom stays at home with their mother. The mother and the young boy go to the Ravine when she worries about her son, but Tom's perception of the danger in the Ravine is removed when Doug returns. Neither mothers, girls, nor younger boys go into the Ravine. Women who go into the Ravine are menaced by a monster-killer called the Lonely One; one woman is killed, and her body is found in the Ravine.

The family and social structures of Green Town reflect the traditional model of sharply defined gender roles. Chores are designated as either for women or for men: women, like Doug's grandmother, do the cooking, while the grandfather, helped by the boys, makes dandelion wine. The sexes often separate for social gatherings: men smoke cigars, while ladies go to the movies together. The wives and mothers tend to stay at home, but all family members mingle on the porches in the evenings.

Women characters are always identified by their martial status. While there are a few bachelor characters, they are not identified as such, just called by their names. The children, with the exception of Tom, a younger boy, tend to play in groups segregated by sex.

Women who step out of traditional roles may suffer negative consequences. When Miss Fern and Miss Roberta run over Mr. Quartermain in their electric car, they retreat quickly to the attic of their house, but Doug saves them from public humiliation. Women like Miss Lavinia

Nebbs or Miss Elizabeth Ramsell (the woman whose body Lavinia finds in the Ravine), who insist on going outside despite rumors of the Lonely One, risk death.

In terms of narrative time and the importance of the male characters, the novel focuses on the masculine world. That focus is shown most strongly in the portrayal of the Lonely One. When Tom and his mother go to the Ravine to search for Doug, she mentions that the Lonely One is around and that nobody is safe (41), although the Lonely One apparently kills only women. Lavinia Nebbs rejects the idea that the threat of the Lonely One should stop her from attending the movies, but she soon finds the body of his latest victim and is menaced herself. She kills an intruder in her house, but the boys' reaction to her act is disappointment. In one of the few times Tom joins Doug and Charlie, the three boys mourn the disappearance of the Lonely One, whose absence will turn their town into "vanilla junket" (178). Only when Tom convinces them that the man killed is just a tramp, on the grounds that the real Lonely One wouldn't look like a normal man, do the boys return to their gleeful excitement over a serial killer menacing their town.

In a novel so concerned with the idea of death and its effect on human beings, a serial killer is thought of and enjoyed like a scary but thrilling movie. While the boys say they don't really wish Lavinia Nebbs had died in her house, the deaths of the women the Lonely One killed do not seem to be as real as the other deaths in the book, although Doug is affected by his near exposure to the Lonely One (he was in the Ravine at about the same time Elizabeth Ramsell was killed). In the terms of a gender reading, *Dandelion Wine* does an excellent job of showing the initiation and maturation of a man in a traditional patriarchal culture, but its theme is not universally applicable to everyone, especially to women.

Something Wicked This Way Comes
(1962)

Something Wicked This Way Comes (*SWTWC*) was published in 1962. The 1997 paperback edition is dedicated to the memory of Gene Kelly, dancer and friend of Bradbury's. The Afterword of the edition describes Bradbury's appreciation of Kelly's work and their friendship. The novel had its genesis in a short story that Bradbury turned into a screen treatment for Kelly. But funding could not be arranged, and so Bradbury turned it into a novel which, some years later, did become a film.

The novel is in some ways a companion to *Dandelion Wine*, also set in Green Town. L. T. Biddison, an academic critic, in "Ray Bradbury's Song of Experience," argues that the main characters of both novels can be read as the same person and as based on Bradbury himself. Biddison analyzes the extent to which the novels "delve . . . into the subconscious—and even unconscious—mind of man," showing that "the adult's world of prosaic and often meaningless fact is not the real world at all" compared to the child's vision of a glorious world (Biddison 226). *SWTWC*, according to Biddison, focuses on the sexual maturing that takes place during early adolescence as well as the relationship between fathers and sons (Biddison 227–29).

PLOT DEVELOPMENT

Something Wicked This Way Comes is set in Green Town, Illinois, in late October. The idyllic nature of Green Town, based on Bradbury's memories of growing up in Waukegan, Illinois, is characterized by small-town values and traditional social roles. The action of the novel takes place within limited time, from late afternoon on a Friday to midnight on the following Sunday, late in the month of October.

SWTWC is structured in three titled sections: "Arrivals" (chapters 1–24), "Pursuits" (chapters 25–44), and "Departures" (chapters 45–54), with a prologue and an afterword. The prologue briefly establishes the time of year, introduces the characters of Jim Nightshade and William Halloway, and explains that what happens in the novel forever changes these two young protagonists. Their age is emphasized: When the novel begins, Jim is thirteen years, eleven months, and twenty-three days old, while Will is thirteen years, eleven months, and twenty-four days old, and both are looking forward to Halloween and to being fourteen.

Chapters 1–10 present the setting, major characters, and conflicts of the novel. The novel begins with a lightning rod salesman named Tom Fury arriving in Green Town. He meets Jim and Will late Friday afternoon and sells them a lightning rod, predicting that a bad storm is going to hit Jim's house. Will and Jim's actions on this Friday evening are normal for these two best friends on an autumn weekend. They race to the library where they visit with Will's father, Charles Halloway, check out books, and run home through the town. The two boys do experience some conflict on the way home when Jim wants to go by a house where, last August, they had seen a naked couple making love, and Will does not. As they walk home, the wind blows them a handbill about a carnival. Meanwhile, Charles closes the library where he works as a janitor and stops at a saloon. Charles sees himself as an old man, envying the youth and energy of Will and Jim.

While at the saloon, Charles sees a man displaying a placard for "Cooger & Dark's Pandemonium Shadow Show," and stops to view a display in an empty shop that promises to exhibit "the Most Beautiful Woman in the World" in a block of ice. Charles and Will are both aware of the promised arrival of the carnival, but they do not tell Will's mother. When Jim arrives home, readers learn that he is an only child, having survived the deaths of two siblings and the loss of his father. Chapter

10 returns to the lightning rod salesman, Tom Fury, who is walking through town after midnight and catches sight of the same display that Charles saw, except that he does see a woman in the ice, a woman as beautiful as the statues he saw in Rome and the paintings he saw in Paris. Tom enters the shop and becomes the first person to disappear from Green Town.

The novel contains a pattern of light and darkness that structures the plot. Chapters 11–14 take place during Friday night, when the promised carnival arrives in a most unusual way: after midnight. Will and Jim are in bed, but are awakened by the sound of a train engine and strange music. They climb out their windows to investigate. They see the train pass over the railway bridge, and they follow it to a large meadow, where they watch the carnival set up. The darkness and strangeness frightens them both, and they run home. Charles is also aware of the carnival arriving. He has gone back to the library, as he often does. When he walks home, he sees in place of the display he saw earlier only a puddle of water with some strange shards and hairs, which he refuses to acknowledge. The chapter ends with Will lying in bed listening to his father return and feeling threatened, and Charles feeling depressed as he often does at three o'clock in the morning.

Chapter 15–17 covers Saturday from dawn to sunset. During this period, the strange and threatening nature of the carnival becomes apparent to Will and Jim. They spend the day at the carnival, which seems, at first, to be normal. But then they have an unsettling experience when they meet Miss Foley, their 7th-grade teacher, who is taking a visiting nephew to the carnival. She insists on going into the Mirror Maze, but then becomes terrified, and Will has to rescue her. Will would like to leave after that, but Jim insists on staying at least until sunset, although he agrees to avoid the Mirror Maze. At sunset, though, Jim disappears and Will must rescue him from the Maze as well. Jim still insists on returning to the carnival after dark, and asks Will to come along. As they start to leave the carnival temporarily, they trip over a bag of lightning rods that they recognize as Tom Fury's. This discovery encourages them to come back and explore, although they are both fearful.

A major turning point of the novel comes in chapter 18, where the fantastic elements that have been only hinted at, never clearly described, manifest themselves to both Jim and Will. The chapter starts with Will and Jim looking at the merry-go-round that has had an "Out of Order" sign posted all day. They've visited the other rides and seen nothing

interesting, so Jim climbs on it. A man working on the carousel catches
Jim, and then Will when he tries to rescue his friend. A second man
orders the first to put them down, and they talk.

The first man is Mr. Cooger, and the second is Mr. Dark; they are the
owners of the carnival. Dark is attracted to Jim, and shows his "illustrations," which are described as different than tattoos. Jim looks at them,
seeing a snake, and seems bewitched. Dark wants to know their names,
but they give false ones. Dark gives them a card for a free ride when the
merry-go-round is fixed, and tells them to come back at seven. The boys
leave, but hide in a tree to watch. They see Dark start the carousel running backward and Cooger leap on it and ride it backward, becoming
younger with each revolution, ending up as a boy of twelve. The boys
agree they have to see more.

The events during the rest of Saturday night are related in chapters
19–31, moving from the "Arrivals" to the "Pursuits" section. The plot
focuses on Dark's attempt to capture the boys, although he seems willing
to seduce Jim into a partnership. After Cooger's transformation on the
merry-go-round, Jim and Will chase after him into town, finding him at
Miss Foley's. They go into the house to talk to Miss Foley, who introduces the boy as her nephew Robert, but whom Will knows to be Cooger
as a child. They cannot say anything to warn Miss Foley because of
Cooger's presence.

When they finally return home, their parents are upset with them and
send them to bed without dinner. Later, Will realizes that Jim is leaving
his room without notifying him, the first time he's tried to leave his
friend behind. Will follows Jim, who goes first to Miss Foley's house to
try to talk to the nephew. Will fights Jim to stop this attempt, but their
fight alerts the nephew, who throws jewelry outside and accuses them
of theft. Then the nephew tries to escape back to the carnival, but they
chase him.

The nephew reaches the merry-go-round and starts to ride it forward
to get older and bigger, and Will fights Jim again to keep him from
jumping on. Their struggle over the control box is interrupted when
lightning hits it, and the carousel goes on a mad ride forward, which
ends with Cooger a fantastic husk of an old man of a hundred or more.
The boys are frightened, but finally call both the police and an ambulance. When they arrive, the boys lead them back into the carnival, but
there is nothing on the carousel. When they go into the main carnival
tent, Mr. Dark explains what the boys saw as a new attraction, Mr. Electrico, the false figure of an old man in an electric chair. Will also sees a

dwarf that he believes is Tom Fury, the lightning rod salesman, crushed into a small figure.

These events conclude chapter 24, the last chapter of the first section, and set up a major complication: the secular authorities, the police and medical institutions, cannot help the boys. The authorities would not believe them in any case, and it is doubtful that they could do anything to oppose Dark and Cooger even if they did believe. The police and the ambulance crew live in another world and are content to wander through the tent laughing at the freaks.

The second section of the novel is titled "Pursuits," and details the numerous attempts made by the carnival people to track down the boys and capture them. Miss Foley, who has been affected by the carnival, takes part in these actions. Although she knows that the accusation of theft is false and that, somehow, her nephew is not exactly her nephew, she is tempted by his unspoken promises of youth, of a ride into a time that is "summer, sweet as clover, honey-grass, and wild mint" (122). Miss Foley succumbs to temptation and calls the police and Charles to accuse Jim and Will of theft.

The boys, returning with the police and ambulance, happen to overhear this accusation as they are hiding outside the police station arguing about what they should do next. When Will hears what Miss Foley says, he goes inside to confess. Afterwards, Charles and the boys walk home together. When they reach the neighboring houses, Jim and Will show Charles the secret ladders they've made by nailing rungs to the side of their homes under the ivy. He is amused and reveals that he did the same thing as a boy, but extracts a promise from them to limit their adventures. After Jim climbs up to bed, Charles says he knows that Will did not steal anything despite his confession. Will considers telling his father what has happened, but refrains, wanting to protect him. Will promises to tell everything in a few days.

Little action occurs in chapter 28, but it relates an important moment between father and son. Charles, at age 54, has said he feels he is too old to be a father. His white hair and age are emphasized throughout the earlier section, and both Will and he doubt whether such an "old man" could protect his son if necessary. In this chapter, the father and son, encouraged by the sweetness of the night, talk: "It was a time to say much but not all. . . . It was the new sweetness of men starting to talk as they must talk" (133).

They debate the nature of good and evil and the relationship between goodness and happiness. After a lengthy discussion, they go inside to bed. Will starts to climb his outside ladder, then dares his father to join him. Charles at first declines, then accepts, and the two climb together: "They swung in and sat upon the sill, same size, same weight, colored same by the stars. . . . for fear of waking God, country, wife, Mom, and hell, they snug-clapped hands to each other's mouths, and sat one instant longer" (139). This moment of shared experience foreshadows their reconciliation at the end of the novel.

Despite the happiness of the moment Will shares with his father, the events of Saturday night are not complete. Will wakes up after only an hour, realizing that the lightning rod has been taken off Jim's house, and then perceiving the approach of something that turns out to be the Dust Witch from the carnival, in a balloon. The Witch marks Jim's house. They had given false names, but the blind Witch is somehow able to sense where they live. The boys wash the slimy, snail-like marking off the roof with the garden hose, but Will still cannot sleep. Eventually he goes out to challenge the Witch directly with his Boy Scout bow and arrow. His purpose is to lure her back and then bring the balloon down to delay her report of their location. He decoys her to a deserted house and, after a struggle during which his bow breaks, is able to pierce the balloon by hand with an arrow.

The last day of the novel, Sunday, dawns, and Jim and Will are going to the police station and to visit Miss Foley. But Miss Foley wakes up early and goes out to get her one free ride on the carousel. On the way to the carnival, Will and Jim find a small girl crying under an oak tree. Will recognizes the little girl as Miss Foley and wants to help her, but Jim does not believe it is her. They go to Miss Foley's house and cannot find her, and on the way back are nearly trapped by a parade from the carnival. When they return to the tree, the little girl is gone. Later, Will comes to believe that the little girl must have given Dark their true first names.

Most of the action in Chapters 32–41 is the ongoing search for, or pursuit of, the boys. Charles spends his day researching the occult, carnivals, possession, and witchcraft. When the boys arrive at the library, the three of them engage in a discussion about their situation that stretches over three chapters. For the first time, Will and Jim tell Charles everything that has happened to them. Charles has found news clippings about circuses and carnivals, all owned by men named Dark and Cooger, which traveled through their area in 1846, 1860, and 1888. Charles reveals his theory that the carnival people have evolved as a kind of predator species alongside humans, but that they are not all-powerful, that they can only successfully prey on the "unconnected fools," people who have no familial or other strong connections with other people.

The group speculates further that the carnival people live off the anguish experienced by people: young people who want to be adults, older people who want to be young. What Dark and Cooger promise is false and empty, and based on the fear humans have of death. As they are discussing the nature of the carnival people, they hear the noise of the library door opening. Charles tells the boys to go hide, and sits down to wait for the confrontation.

Chapters 41–44 relate how Dark confronts Charles first, scoffing at his attempts to research the carnival and offering him his youth again if he identifies the boys. Charles refuses, determined to protect Will and Jim. Dark then searches the library, first trying to tempt them out by offering Jim a ride on the merry-go-round and saying that they've spun Will's mother into extreme old age. This attempt fails, but Dark tracks them down, lying on top of the shelves. The Dust Witch enchants them into living statues who cannot see, speak, or hear. Dark wounds Charles's left arm and takes the boys with him, leaving the Witch to kill Charles by stopping his heart. The final chapter of the section relates how Charles, almost by accident, discovers the only thing that successfully halts the Witch: laughter. He survives, drives her away, and goes out to rescue Will and Jim.

The last nine chapters of the novel, comprising the last section titled "Departures," relate how Charles and Will are finally able to defeat Dark and Cooger. Dark takes Will and Jim back to the carnival. Again, Dark offers Jim the chance to become a partner if Cooger doesn't survive, but he plans to ride Will on the merry-go-round back to infancy and give him to the Dwarf to carry. After they arrive back at the carnival, Dark puts the two boys in the waxworks behind the Mirror Maze until the carnival closes. He then goes off to orchestrate the last event: the Bullet Trick. When the Dust Witch returns and tell him that Charles is not dead, he makes her stand on the stage to catch the bullet in her teeth. At first there is no volunteer to fire the rifle, but then Charles arrives and volunteers.

Charles calls for Will to help him; when the crowd joins in, Will is able to move from the waxworks to the stage, although he cannot talk or move on his own. Charles makes sure a crescent moon is carved into the bullet (both the real one, and the wax one that Dark replaces it with), and then balances the rifle on Will's shoulder. The Witch is killed by the bullet because it bears Charles's smile, although Dark pretends she has fainted. Dark turns out the lights to close the carnival down, and Will and Charles try to rescue Jim. When the Witch is killed, Will is freed completely, and Jim partially. Will and Charles go into the Mirror Maze to get Jim and are nearly defeated when Charles is frightened by the images of old men he sees around him. Will helps rescue him, first through light (matches) and then by telling his father that he loves him no matter what. Charles is able to laugh, which destroys the Mirror Maze. But Jim is no longer in the waxworks; he has left, still fascinated by the idea of growing up fast, for the merry-go-round, where the final confrontation takes place.

Dark tries one last time to take Cooger/Mr. Electrico to the merry-go-round to spin him young again. Jim blocks them and Cooger is destroyed when his chair falls to the ground. Rather than continuing to fight Dark, Jim grabs a pole on the carousel and starts to go around. Will tries to pull him off by the one hand that Jim has extended to him. The boys go once or twice around before Will succeeds in pulling him off. Jim seems dead, and as they try to help him, a boy runs up crying for help. Charles goes with him but recognizes Dark, accuses him, and draws him close, just holding him and refusing to give him the power of Charles's fear.

Dark is finally destroyed by these actions. After he is dead, his tattoos vanish, which frees the rest of the carnival people. Will begins to mourn the loss of his friend, but Charles realizes that Jim can be healed by laughter and singing. The father and son, singing and dancing crazily, revive Jim. Before they leave, they face one final temptation as they think about taking only a few rides on the merry-go-round. But they realize that one ride would inevitably lead them to becoming the new owners of the carnival, so they destroy the carousel forever. Then the three of them race home in the moonlight, the two boys running together again as friends and Charles running even with them, perceiving himself to be a middle-aged man rather than old (and near death).

CHARACTER DEVELOPMENT

The novel is narrated in the third-person omniscient point of view, a narrative point of view that stands outside the story rather than taking a character's perspective. The third-person narrative point of view is able to report on the actions, dialogue, and thoughts or emotions of any or all of the characters, although most third-person narratives tend to focus on several major point of view characters. The major point of view characters in *SWTWC* are Will and Charles Halloway. Will is the single or major point of view character in twenty chapters, Charles in twelve.

Since the narrative structure describes events that take place at two or three locations simultaneously, the point of view must shift, sometimes quickly, between or within chapters. In nine chapters the perspective shifts between the various point of view characters, sometimes including three or four perspectives. In three chapters the perspective focuses on Will and Jim together; in these chapters they act and respond as one being, and the narrative point of view is reported as "they." Other characters are the point of view characters only at key points: Tom Fury and Jim in two chapters, Miss Foley in one.

The two characters whose thoughts and emotions we learn the most about are Will and Charles, and they also undergo the most change in their perceptions of the world and of each other. Characters such as Tom Fury and Miss Foley serve important functions without changing: Tom as the messenger who warns the boys of the oncoming storm and as the first "unconnected" person trapped by the carnival, Miss Foley as an important figure in the boys' lives who is seduced by the carnival's promises.

Will and Jim are described in the first chapter from the point of view of Tom Fury, the lightning rod salesman. He sees that Will has "milk-blonde hair" and eyes that are "bright and clear as a drop of summer rain," while Jim has hair "wild, thick, and the glossy color of waxed chestnuts. His eyes . . . were mint rock-crystal green" (6). The two boys have been neighbors and best friends all their lives. Will was born a minute before midnight on October 30 and Jim one minute later, on Halloween. Even in the first few pages of the novel, the two boys, one light and one dark, are distinguished. Will can hardly wait to install the lightning rod on Jim's house, but Jim doesn't want to spoil the fun and is reluctant to act until Will reminds him of his mother.

Both Will and Jim are aware of their differences. In chapter 9, Jim meditates on how they see the world. Jim has seen more than Will, and is too aware of the death that comes to everyone. The two want different things as well, or at least want them at a different time. Their different responses to seeing a naked couple engaged in sexual intercourse show their different levels of maturity, as do their responses to the carnival. Will always tries to oppose Dark and Cooger, but Jim is tempted by the carousel from the start. Throughout the novel, Jim never gives up wanting that ride to physical adulthood, to what he perceives as the greater freedom that adults have. Jim does finally reject the temptation, enough to reach out to Will in order to be rescued at the end.

But the two are also best friends and very similar not only in their birthdates. They are boys: "Like all boys, they never walked anywhere, but named a goal and lit for it, scissors and elbows. . . . Nobody wanted to win. . . . they just wanted to run forever, shadow and shadow" (12). They have spent years perfecting a system for communicating—dancing out tunes on an old boardwalk that Will's grandfather had preserved by moving it to an alley—that lets each one signal the other to join in a night's adventure.

The plot of the novel sets them in conflict over the carnival; at the start, Will gives way to Jim, who seems the stronger of the two, always telling him yes and going along with him. But Will is the one who rescues Miss Foley, Jim, and Charles from the Mirror Maze, and then pulls Jim off the carousel—although, as Charles makes clear, Jim participates in his own rescue.

Another important relationship between characters is the father-son relationship. Will sees his father as extra protection between himself and the darkness that Jim does not have. At the start of the novel, however, Charles does not see himself as able to protect his son because of age. Charles changes and grows in his own and Will's estimation through the course of the novel: he rejects Dark's offer of false youth and goes on to save the boys. Will comes to a new understanding of his father as well. As they talk together after the confession at the police station, and when he sees his father driving Dark and the Witch away, and when they talk in the library, Will grows into an awareness of his father that, at the end, lets them rescue each other from the dark.

The antagonists who oppose Charles and Will are Dark and Cooger, the owners of the carnival. Dark is tall and pale, with "licorice black" hair and yellow eyes, and wears a suit that seems to be bristly and itching (73). Cooger has "flame-red hair, bright flame-blue eyes" (75). Two men opposed to the two boys—both pairs with dark and light coloring. The similarity is made apparent at the start, although it might be more accurate to call them mirror images of the boys, reversed rather than true images. Dark and Cooger are partners, but neither seems willing to go to the lengths for each other that Will does for Jim. In fact, Dark is ready to recruit Jim as a new partner if Cooger does not survive.

The major characters, both the protagonists and the antagonists, are all men. Only four women are mentioned: Mrs. Halloway (Charles's wife and Will's mother); Mrs. Nightshade (Jim's mother); Miss Foley, the boys' spinster schoolteacher; and the Dust Witch, one of the carnival people. Little or no description is given of the women, and they appear only briefly.

THEMES

The major theme is related to the genre Bradbury has chosen: horror or gothic. The overall plot device of the everyday world being affected by a dark, supernatural force is common in gothic novels and a favorite convention of Bradbury's. *SWTWC* is an excellent example of a gothic story. A Midwestern town, two adolescents, and a carnival could have been a nostalgic view of an idyllic past, similar to *Dandelion Wine* in tone. Bradbury's tale of spiritual predators who feast off human anguish at the normal processes of life, and who evoke even more anguish by making false promises of eternal youth, turns these nostalgic elements into a suspenseful and horrifying story.

The themes of the story are the spiritual conflict between good and evil—specifically, the goodness of ordinary people, who love family and community, against the evil of the isolated predators, who can band together with others but cannot love. There is little direct violence; instead, the autumn people, the carnival people, play on human fears through a kind of symbolic magic, perhaps because they feed on spiritual anguish rather than physical pain. Charles and Will cannot use physical action against their opponents because it does not work (when forced, Dark is able to physically harm Charles). Instead, Charles and Will learn that laughter, a laughter based on knowledge of people and life, and the emotional connections humans make with each other, primarily through family ties, are the response that robs the predators of their power.

The good-versus-evil theme of the novel is shown not only in the plot and characters, but in Bradbury's poetic style, in which images carry symbolic or abstract messages. The imagery—words that describe the physical world as experienced through the five senses (touch, taste, smell, sight, and hearing)—works throughout the novel to reinforce the theme.

The novel's first image presented is that of the storm, especially lightning. Tom Fury, with his lighting rods and storm-colored clothing, is the first character introduced, and the carnival arrives with the storm, which is also associated with autumn. The storm is not necessarily allied with the evil of the carnival; lightning hitting the control box of the merry-go-round results in Cooger's becoming extremely old. When Will battles the Witch on the roof, the wind seems to be trying to help him oppose her balloon. The storm imagery, images from the natural world, can, perhaps by coincidence, work for either "good" or "evil."

The second major cluster of images (see discussion of image clusters in Chapter 5) of is that of light and dark, from the blond hair and light eyes of Will versus the dark chestnut hair and dark eyes of Jim. Jim is more drawn to the shadows of the carnival and so is more at risk. Light and dark are also seen in the opposition of night and day, with the night associated with the forces of evil and day with the forces of good. Day and night clearly structure the novel's time and plot; the hours from midnight to three o'clock in the morning are particularly open for evil to reign unchecked, whereas sunrise brings some relief for the boys.

A third major image cluster is related to water in its various forms. Frozen water symbolizes time, which can kill a human. The block of ice with the invisible mermaid and the Mirror Maze as a cold devouring sea show the mirror aspect of water. The linking of mirrors with water, and thus negatively with the passage of time, is clearly made in chapter 25, where Miss Foley is said to have ignored the "bright shadows of herself" (in mirrors) for some time. Mirrors are described as "cold sheets of December ice in the hall, above the bureaus, in the bath. Best skate the thin ice, lightly. Paused, the weight of your attention might crack the shell. Plunged through the crust, you might drown" (121).

ALTERNATIVE PERSPECTIVES: A FEMINIST READING

Feminist literary criticism has brought a specific set of questions to literary analysis, focusing on how women are represented in literature. Feminist critics bring questions about the social and historical context of literature to bear, as well as examining the extent to which representations of women in literature perpetuate social and cultural stereotypes. While feminist criticism is a large and complex area in which questions of ethnicity, class, and sexuality have also come into play, some of the earliest points made by feminist critics can be used to develop a reading of how this novel presents women. The extent to which female characters are presented only in relationship to male characters, and the resulting tendency to see female characters as positive or negative because of their relationship with male characters, is stronger in gothic or horror fiction because of the genre conventions. Hazel Pierce, a scholar who places

Bradbury's novels in the genre of gothic novels rather than science fiction, notes, women writers developed the gothic convention of young, innocent women who were in danger because of sexual decadence. Horror stories tend to present women as either victims or villains.

Bradbury, in *SWTWC*, focuses on innocent (or fairly innocent) adolescent boys. The boys' relationships with adult men—notably, Charles Halloway, Dark, and Cooger—initiate the process of becoming "men" as opposed to boys. Charles presents the cultural belief that men are completely different beings than women because of the differences in reproductive abilities. In chapter 14 he looks at his sleeping wife and muses that a woman can have true immortality through childbearing, while men cannot really believe they are fathers: "what father ever really believes it? He carries no burden, he feels no pain. What man, like woman, lies down in darkness and gets up with child? The gentle, smiling ones own the good secret. . . . Why speak of Time when you *are* Time, and shape the universal moments. . . . ?" (58–59). This image of women is mythic, something other than human. The image also defines women as essentially requiring to bear children to be completely women and, in traditional societies, to marry men rather than to exercise this mysterious power on their own. Charles's musings also go to the heart of what some feminist critics believe is the reason for social restrictions on women: that men, not able to have conclusive proof that their children are in fact their children, need to control other men's access to "their" women.

The novel's main characters are all men, and women play limited roles. The earliest images of women in the novel are not real women at all, but pictures, images, and objects. The first representation of a woman is the poster advertising "The Most Beautiful Woman in the World," and the ice block in which Charles sees an empty space that is somehow a woman (in potential?), and in which the lightning rod salesman sees the shape of a woman that, taking substance from the images of women in art and film, lures him into a trap. In this representation, the woman resembles a siren or mermaid, mythical women in water who lure men to their deaths.

The second woman is a character diametrically opposed to the temptress in the ice block. Will's mother (her first name is never given) is usually shown safe in her home, the one father and son return to after their adventures. Will compares her to a "creamy pink hothouse rose poised alone in the wilderness. . . . smelling like fresh milk, happy, to herself, in this room" (34). The association of women with roses in British and American literature is centuries old; the additional sense impression of milk, which a woman can produce from her body to feed her child, also shows the positive nature of Will's mother. Jim's mother is also described briefly, as someone who wants to keep Jim in the house rather than let him stray outside into danger.

Both mothers are mostly portrayed in the house and in their roles as mothers. The perspective is wholly that of the child, who knows only "Mom" rather than a woman's name. However, these women have a power or stability that most male characters lack. Late in the novel, when Jim and Will have been captured by Dark, all three see Will and Jim's mothers walking home from church. Dark tries to orchestrate a meeting and capture them as well, but fails. The women turn away, perhaps because they are coming from church, perhaps because they are together, or perhaps because mothers, by their nature (according to Charles), are completely fulfilled, not "unconnected fools" who can be trapped by time. The portrayal of mothers is not completely positive: Will describes Jim's mother, who lost her husband, as suffocating Jim because she wants to keep him safe; her love and desire make him want to run away, perhaps to adulthood (93).

The other two female characters in the novel are Miss Foley, the boys' spinster schoolteacher, and the Dust Witch, one of the carnival people. Miss Foley is tempted by the nephew's promise that a carousel ride will restore her to youth. The temptation leads her to lay false charges against the two boys, who are among her favorite students. The Dust Witch is essentially an instrument controlled by Dark, but she is described as a blind, poisonous witch who can cast spells.

Considering the ways in which the female characters are constructed in the context of social expectations of women and in the context of genre conventions can lead to a reading of the way they mirror three deeply rooted archetypes of women: virgin (or spinster), mother, and crone (witch). While feminist writers have claimed these identities as having power for women, *SWTWC* tends to assign simplistic stereotypes to each character type: the mother is presented as positive, but the "virgin" and the "crone" are both negative. Only the woman who fulfills her socially expected role is safe from the threats of Dark and Cooger. Miss Foley is easily tempted, falls, and then, as a little girl, is probably captured by the carnival to become like the Dust Witch, completely evil and dominated by Dark.

Bradbury's novel, while enlarging the focus on the relationship between sons and fathers, reduces the women characters to little more than stereotypes; whether of good or evil, it hardly seems to matter because of the limited roles they have to play.

8

Death Is a Lonely Business
(1985)

Death Is a Lonely Business (DLB) was Bradbury's first novel published since *Something Wicked This Way Comes,* a gap of twenty-three years. Bradbury's move to mystery fiction, while not a new genre for him since he had published a number of mystery and suspense stories in pulp magazines during the 1940s, brought a variety of responses from reviewers. Some praised the novel, while others criticized it. In a 1985 review, critic Paul Barber notes that "readers will see that [Bradbury] is still engaged in his lifelong quest for a literary form that will stand still for the demands that he puts on it. . . . His interest is . . . in finding, somehow, a means of breaking through the limitations of space and time and form, a way of saying the ineffable. . . . where the characters can't go, the images will." Barber realizes that Bradbury "uses the conventions of the detective novel to create something that is profoundly, fundamentally different from the detective novel," and praises the poetic images, vital characters, and vivid description (Barber 1).

Brian Sibley, writing in the *Los Angeles Times,* praises the horror elements of the novel: "the more terrifying because it is centered upon minutely observed life. . . . there will be [readers], horror-hungry, who will relish this nerve-freezing confection" (Sibley 36). As Sibley notes, some readers do not appreciate Bradbury's work: a review printed in *Kirkus Reviews* characterizes the narrator and plot as "soft-boiled," and condemns the "superficial use of [the] murder mystery format." Unlike Barber and Sibley, this reviewer characterizes the novel as a "YA [Young

Adult]-ish fantasy," as "cute and gushy," and as having "quirky blend-
ings of creepiness and humor, innocence and decadence, nightmare and
cartoon" ("Review" *Kirkus Reviews* 799).

The disagreement among critics seems to echo the debate about Bradbury's science fiction, focusing on how he uses the conventions of a popular genre, whose market depends to a great extent on writers following
the conventions, while simultaneously bringing in conventions from
other genres, all the while adding his own blend of poetry and a writer's
observations on American life. This novel is one of three semiautobiographical works that draw on Bradbury's life during the late 1940s and
early 1950s instead of on his childhood. The other two novels in this
group are *A Graveyard for Lunatics* (discussed in chapter 9) and *Green
Shadows, White Whale* (discussed in chapter 10).

While reviewers are careful not to give away the solution to murder
mysteries, readers should note that the following literary analysis does
reveal the name and nature of the murderer.

PLOT DEVELOPMENT

While most of the *DLB*'s events can be summarized in a fairly straight-
forward manner, Bradbury's creation of a writer-narrator who is "telling" the story and the other characters in the novel result in a complexly
layered plot structure. In effect, two plot lines combine to create the
overall structure of the novel. The first plot is the mystery plot; the second is about a writer who writes mysteries (and horror and fantasies).
This second plot could be described as the "Great American Novelist"
plot.

The mystery plot opens one dark night on a trolley, when the narrator
has an encounter with what he believes is a drunk who speaks myste-
riously about death. When the narrator returns home, he discovers a
body stuffed in a lion cage that was dumped in the canal near his home.
As the police investigate, the narrator takes some wet paper found in
the victim's pockets. He starts to investigate and becomes convinced he
met the murderer. While he has some difficulty at first persuading Elmo
Crumley, the police lieutenant in charge of the case, to accept his help,
his identification of the paper as trolley transfers convinces Crumley to
include him in the investigation. The narrator and Crumley soon become
targets of a frightening kind of harassment: a stormy presence outside

their doors late at night that leaves water or seaweed along with wet footprints and a lingering sense of fear and despair.

Other people die, and the narrator and Crumley investigate, with the help of Constance and Henry. While the narrator does not know all the victims, he knows most of them fairly well. His knowledge of the people leads him to find the clues to identify A. L. Shrank as the murderer. On another dark night, he confronts Shrank and elicits a confession. The nature of the murders comes out: Shrank never killed anyone through physical violence, only through manipulation and a version of emotional blackmail and intimidation. He frightened them to death, or into disappearing. He tried to intimidate the narrator and Crumley the same way, but they were able to resist the despair because of their success in writing. Shrank claims that his efforts led to peace for the victims, who were suffering. The confrontation between the narrator and Shrank ends when the narrator tells him that there is one last "Lonely," or empty one, to kill: himself. On hearing that, Shrank jumps into the water, then leaps out and drags the narrator in with him. They fight underwater, and the narrator pushes him into the same lion cage in which the first victim was found. There Shrank finally dies.

Interwoven with the mystery plot is the writing plot. This plot is what twists the conventions of the mystery genre and what makes the novel so recognizably a part of Bradbury's "fantastic" writing. This plot starts with the writer suffering from writer's block. He had been selling stories for pulp magazines for thirty or forty dollars a story. But he hasn't written anything since trying to start the "Great American Novel" on July 1, 1949, the same day that Peg (his fiancée and probably his muse) left to study in Mexico. Events motivate him to start to write again; he writes about the people he meets and talks to during the investigation. During the course of the novel, the narrator receives a letter from the *American Mercury* offering to publish one of his stories for $300, an entirely different level of publishing. This event is similar to Bradbury's shift from publishing in the pulp magazines to publishing in the "slicks" for more money.

Elmo Crumley, the police detective, turns out to be a writer who has also been blocked on his novel. The narrator encourages him to write, even giving him a title for his novel: the words the narrator heard from the man on the trolley he believes is the murderer. The narrator had planned to use it for his own novel, but he gives the title to Crumley as a gift and says he can find another for his own book. The narrator makes Crumley promise to get up and start writing before anything else. And it works; Crumley starts writing regularly, and then finishes his book in a marathon session. His finishing the manuscript scares off the murderer, who had been leaving water and seaweed outside his door at night. Crumley and the narrator realize that their happiness and success has scared away the murderer.

The two plots of the novel come together in the character of the narrator, but they also come together in the question of how one lives life: by thinking rationally about facts or by feeling and intuiting. The narrator believes too much thinking is bad—for writing, for living, and apparently for solving murders. He makes no attempt at the usual kind of investigation found in mysteries; he doesn't collect alibis or look at any clues except the ones involving paper—the trolley ticket punchouts, torn up notes, tabloids. Crumley is the advocate of facts and rationality; he keeps demanding material proof from the narrator that the deaths are anything but accidents. The debate over how to conduct an investigation turns into the question of how to write.

By the end of the novel, the narrator has "won" both debates; he is correct that the deaths are not accidental, and he discovers the murderer. Both the narrator and Elmo Crumley break out of their cases of writer's block and succeed in their projects. The novel the narrator is writing during the course of the novel turns out, in a circular structure, to be the novel that we are reading. Crumley eventually publishes his novel as well (described in *A Graveyard for Lunatics*).

The writer's plot also connects to an element of the novel that Bradbury is known for in his other work. This element is the attention paid to describing the lives of people. In a traditional mystery plot, events arise out of earlier events, that is, they are caused by those earlier events. Characters, to a certain extent, serve the plot's needs. In the writer's plot, the focus is on characters rather than specific events. The interactions of the various characters in Venice and Los Angeles, some of whom the narrator already knows and some of whom he meets during the course of investigating the murder, are what interest the writer. These characters form their own kinds of communities within the larger urban setting: the inhabitants and owners of attractions on the pier (Shapeshade, Annie Oakley, and Shrank), the inhabitants of the Los Angeles tenement (Fannie Florianna, Sam, Jimmy, Pietro, and Henry) and the film community (Constance and Hopwood). These communities show the diversity of cultures in Los Angeles during the 1940s.

Both plots depend on the presence of books in the narrative. Books are clues for the writer-narrator as well as being his business. When the narrator first sees Shrank's library on the pier, he assigns a certain meaning to it, and then must revise his understanding of what the library means. At first sight, the narrator is impressed by the sight of so many books and the fact that Shrank can tell him exactly how many books he owns. However, what the narrator fails to notice—the exact nature of those books—turns out to be one of the major clues: "That dreadful escarpment inhabited by dooms, that lineup of failures, that literary Apocalypse of wars, squalors, diseases, pestilences, depressions, that downfall of nightmares, that pit of deliriums and mazes. . . . this was no library, it was an abattoir, a dungeon, a tower" (260).

In this book about murder, literature is one of the most important elements. Literature is explicitly referred to in the novel in two ways: the literary allusions made by the characters and the books associated with Shrank. The narrator and Crumley (between the two of them) allude to Thomas Mann's *Death in Venice*, Hemingway, and Pope. Hopwood tries to bribe the narrator with the chance of meeting Aldous Huxley, and the narrator's response shows how much he is tempted, almost to madness, because of his admiration for Huxley's work and wit. The narrator describes Shrank's library as containing books with depressing themes: *The Decline and Fall of the Roman Empire*, *Suicide as an Answer*, *The Red Sun Rises*, *The Anatomy of Melancholy*, and books written by Friedrich Nietzsche, Arthur Schopenhauer, Edgar Allan Poe, Mary Shelley, Sigmund Freud, Shakespeare's tragedies, Marquis de Sade, Eugene O'Neill, and others.

CHARACTER DEVELOPMENT

The novel is told in the first person by the protagonist, a writer of pulp fiction who is twenty-seven years old. The real name of the narrator-protagonist is never given, although characters address him by various nicknames, including "the Crazy." However, the narrator is clearly based on Bradbury himself. The most significant hint to the narrator's identity within the novel is his regular summary of stories that he has written in the past. Readers familiar with Bradbury's stories will recognize all of them, although the titles are never given. However, *DLB* is a novel, with some fantastic elements, and must be distinguished from an autobiography: readers cannot assume that events in the novel took place as described.

First-person narrators are characters within the stories they tell, and they have the same limits that people do in their everyday lives; that is, a first-person narrator can describe his own thoughts, feelings, actions, and speech as well as the actions and dialogue of other characters. Since this novel has a mystery that the protagonist has already solved and is describing in the past tense, the narrator knows more than the reader. But as with most first-person narratives, the narrator tries to re-create his own perceptions of the events as they took place. Even with that attempt, there is always a certain level of self-conscious reflection and, in the case of a murder mystery, the planting of certain clues that readers may or may not pick up on during their first reading.

The unnamed writer is single and lives in a one-room apartment in Venice, California, supporting himself by his writing. He has published stories in periodicals such as *Dime Detective* and *Black Mask*, for what Bradbury remembers earning per story himself at this time: thirty to forty dollars. Since he doesn't make much, his studio apartment is sparsely furnished. A typewriter contains a sheet of paper with "UN-TITLED NOVEL," his name, and a date three months earlier typed on it. This writer is suffering from writer's block, brought on by his girlfriend being away in Mexico, or perhaps by the three months of rain. His discovery of the first dead body inspires him to start writing again, specifically a novel titled "Death Is a Lonely Business" (15).

The writer-protagonist is not a character who would exist in the hard-boiled mystery fiction that Bradbury admires: this character chews spearmint gum (rather than smoking cigarettes) and consumes candy rather than booze. In fact, he tells Elmo Crumley that he'd rather have chocolate malts than beer or other alcoholic drinks. The traditional hard-boiled detective tends to be older, or at least more worldly wise, cynical, hard-drinking, and averse to marriage (but not against sexual liaisons with the women he meets). The protagonist of *Death Is a Lonely Business* is faithful to his absent girlfriend (who becomes his fiancée during the course of the novel) even when faced with the sexual temptations offered by Constance Rattigan, an older but still gorgeous reclusive film star who enjoys swimming in the nude.

Peg, the narrator's girlfriend, has a presence in the novel even though she is in Mexico. She and the narrator talk to each other at regular intervals; he has to use the pay phone outside his building. She sends him a photograph when he is afraid he cannot remember exactly what she looks like, and partway through, she proposes to him since he's been avoiding proposing to her because of his lack of money.

The other major characters in the novel tend to go against the conventions of popular mystery fiction. The police detective, Lieutenant Elmo

Crumley, seems fairly traditional at first. He rejects any attempts by an amateur to help solve the murder. However, Crumley soon reveals himself to be well read in literary classics and to be passionately attached to gardening. He can quote or refer to writers as diverse as Ernest Hemingway, Feodor Dostoevesky, and Alexander Pope. In addition, Crumley is writing his own novel and suffering from writer's block. He lives in a house surrounded by an exotic garden, where he cultivates African plants.

Another major character is Constance Rattigan, the reclusive film star from the 1920s, who helps the narrator solve the mystery. The narrator spends time staring at her house, which is close to his apartment, and imagines her life as a mysterious recluse. When they finally meet, he tells her he expected to see "someone like Norma Desmond in that movie that just came out" (136). The reference here is to Billy Wilder's 1950 film *Sunset Boulevard* about an aging silent film star, Norma Desmond, who becomes involved with a young writer. Bradbury's narrator's relationship with Constance is as unlike that film as Constance is unlike Norma, but the reference shows how the narrator sees life as similar to movies. He expected an unhappy, obsessive, perhaps alcoholic, woman clinging to her past and trying to recreate it. Instead, she is a vital woman, suntanned and gorgeous, who swims constantly, gave up her film career for what she considers good reason (disgust with the studio system and business), and continues to act by "playing" her chauffeur and maid.

The third important character who helps the narrator solve the murder is Henry (no last name is given). Henry lives in the tenement where the narrator once had a room. He is African American and blind, but is one of the most capable characters in the novel. Henry eventually helps the narrator by loaning him money, recognizing the "smell" of the murderer from earlier visits to the tenement, and helping the narrator track the murderer down and confront him at a pier. Henry also brings Crumley and the police to help the narrator at the end.

Other characters are minor in terms of narrative time, but they are important to the protagonist: these characters are the people he has met and come to care about over the years. They are different in age, gender, and background, but they all have one thing in common: they are eccentric, refusing to conform to social expectations. These characters include friends who live in a tenement five miles from Venice and a group of business owners whose businesses on the Venice Pier are scheduled to be destroyed. They are a reclusive opera singer, known by her stage name Fannie Florianna; Cal, a barber who gives the worst haircuts in the world; a "practicing psychologist" with five thousand books named A. L. Shrank; Mr. Shapeshade, a theater owner; and Annie Oakley, who owns a shooting gallery.

The final group of characters are the ostensible victims of the murderer: this group includes people the narrator does not know by name as well as some of his friends. The murderer describes his victims as the "Lonelies," and the narrator sees them as having failed or having been disappointed in some important way. The victims are a retired trolley operator; a bedridden elderly woman who kept canaries; Cal the barber (who disappears); Pietro, who lives with dozens of animals he rescued; Sam and Jimmy from the tenement; Fannie; and Constance Rattigan, who disappears along with another retired film star, John Wilkes Hopwood. Not all the victims die: Cal returns home to his family; Constance hides out before returning to help the narrator solve the crime. But most die or are irretrievably harmed. All the victims live alone and seem to lack some social connection, which makes them vulnerable to the murderer.

The murderer is present from the start of the novel but not identified as the murderer until the end. The murderer is first introduced as an anonymous shape on the trolley. Late at night, a drunk tells the narrator (who tries to ignore him) that death is a lonely business. By the end of the novel, the narrator learns that the murderer has been tracking him, considering him a potential victim until he started selling his stories and fell in love with Peg, which made him no longer one of the "Lonelies." After the murderer stops thinking of the writer as a potential victim, he uses him to track other victims. The murderer turns out to be A. L. Shrank, the practicing psychologist, who lives in a shack on the pier, surrounded by exactly "five thousand nine hundred and ten books" (67).

The narrator and Shrank are presented as similar but opposing characters throughout the novel. At the beginning, both Crumley and Constance suspect or at least wonder whether the narrator is the one hurting or killing people. Fannie believes the narrator, although a close friend of hers, could bring death to her. The narrator writes stories that, based on his descriptions, embody terrifying themes about the loss of love, life, and identity. Shrank is a bibliophile (book lover) who lives in the midst of 5,910 books about death, depression, and the loss of self. The two share a single trolley ride together at the beginning of the novel; at the end, Shrank tells him that he followed him around to discover new victims. The narrator-writer goes around to collect people for his books, while Shrank collects them for his murder plot. Both the narrator and Shrank maintain a certain distance from people: the narrator because he uses people as the basis for his characters, and Shrank because he sets them up to die. Finally, the narrator, suffering writer's block, is moved to write a novel using the words the murderer said to him at the start as the title: "Death Is a Lonely Business."

SETTING

The setting of *DLB* is Venice, California, in 1949. The narrator describes the town in the context of the myth of the frontier West (and the 1849 gold rush in California) that has not played out: "this far lost end of the continent, where the trail wagons had stopped and the people with them" (6). At the beginning of the novel, in a bar, the barman is watching a Hopalong Cassidy movie on television. Venice is a part of Los Angeles, part of the landscape explored by Raymond Chandler and other writers of hard-boiled mysteries. Certain locations in Venice and Los Angeles are important: the narrator's studio apartment; the pier (with its attendant rides and booths), which is being torn down throughout the novel; Constance Rattigan's house; and a Los Angeles tenement where the narrator-protagonist used to live.

THEMES

The major theme of *Death Is a Lonely Business* is how we live life, a life that leads, inevitably, to death. Specifically, the connections between people, which involve various kinds of love and friendship, and the creation of art or gardens or films, artifacts that might live beyond the life of the creator, are important parts of life. Life, because of time, is linked to death. This theme is embodied in the major symbols of the novel, which embody life and death as well as time.

One of the most important symbols is water. Water surrounds the narrator: the Pacific Ocean lies to the west of his apartment, and the Venice canals to the east. Water is a complex symbol that can carry multiple meanings, life and death. East and west, the directions of the rising and setting sun, tend to be associated with birth and death as well, so the combination of directions and water emphasizes that cycle. The first body is found in a lion cage, under water, and the novel ends with the final struggle between Shrank and the narrator under water in the same lion cage, bringing the narrative full circle. Constance's beach house gives her easy access to the ocean for swimming, which is, for her, protection and life. Venice's heavy fogs and mists bring water onto the land as well.

Dinosaur fossils are another important symbol related to time. The narrator describes the roller coaster, the oil wells, and the old woman who used to sell canaries as dinosaur fossils. Dinosaur fossils suggest something of great size and power that is now extinct. Fossils represent death, but a death that leaves imprints or images that survive the death of the individual being.

ALTERNATE PERSPECTIVE: A POSTMODERN READING

The terms "Postmodernism," "Poststructuralism," and "Deconstruction" are complex and broad terms that describe movements in America that developed in the late 1960s and have affected a number of academic and intellectual disciplines. Certain key theorists are associated with the movement: Jacques Derrida, Julia Kristeva, Roland Barthes, Jean Baudrillard, and Michel Foucault. American literary scholars such as Paul de Man, J. Hillis Miller, and Barbara Johnson argued for including these European movements in American literary theory.

These movements share a rejection of modernist ideas about how knowledge is constructed, how meaning is made, and how viewers or readers understand texts. With regard to postmodern literary criticism, postmodernists and poststructuralists argue against any universal meaning that transcends, or is separate from, language. In practical terms, "deconstructing" a text is based on the assumption that "a text has multiple interpretations and that it allows itself to be reread and thus reinterpreted countless times," and that "[u]ltimately, a text's meaning is undecidable" (Bressler 129).

One poststructural concept can be applied particularly to Bradbury's *Death Is a Lonely Business*: the concept expressed by Michel Foucault in his essay "What Is an Author?" (Davis and Schleifer). Foucault's essay analyzes the different concepts and meaning assigned to the word "author," which means more than just the proper name of the person who is believed to be the one who produced a text. The "author" is also a function—partly a function of privilege (as compared to "writers," authors create "literature") and partly of classification. The function of the author changes over time and varies among different cultures, so there is no single or simple meaning for the word "author." Foucault traces different meanings through several centuries, analyzing the different functions associated with authors assigned to different categories (such as "sacred," "scientific," "poetic," etc.).

Critics and reviews that focus more on *Death Is a Lonely Business* as a "murder mystery" ignore its autobiographical elements. The book is the first of three autobiographical texts in which Bradbury the "author" presents himself as an adult character, not as the child of his earlier autobiographical fantasies. Read as a murder mystery, this novel breaks some conventional rules to focus more on characters and images as well as fantastic elements.

However, the novel can also be read as a postmodern text, one in which the author, "Ray Bradbury," whose name appears on the title page of the novel, deconstructs the notions of the author as a stable figure and genres as simple categories. Within the pages of the book (a material object which can be purchased), the Narrator of the novel, who never gives his "proper name," is engaged in writing a novel that he titles *Death Is a Lonely Business* after his first encounter with the murderer (15). Both the actual novel published by "Bradbury" the author and the novel being written by the Narrator of the story have the same title.

The extent to which Bradbury deconstructs the genre boundaries is shown in how the mystery plot is not resolved in any way that will be familiar to readers of the genre. The lack of closure at the end, the questions about the murderer's chosen victims, the lack of reliance upon clues, the transformation of the police lieutenant into a writer, and the fact that successful completion of novels save the Narrator and Elmo Crumley from the midnight visitations are all ways in which Bradbury deconstructs mystery conventions and focuses on writing based on a shifting sense of self. Additionally, the novel's insistence that stories about life and death ("murder mysteries") need to be considered in close association with other texts about life and death ("literature"), shown by the literary knowledge of the Narrator and Elmo Crumley, is another way in which genre conventions and relative status are dissolved.

A large portion of the novel is autobiographical in nature. The Narrator's life in Venice, California, the stories he writes (and sells) during the course of the novel, his fiancée, and his sudden breakthrough from selling to pulp magazines to being published in the glossy mainstream magazines are all also part of the biographical information published about Bradbury. No sources about Bradbury's life include his solving a number of murders during this time, however, so those elements are

part of the mystery plot. Refusing to assign a proper name to the character of the Narrator and building in the multiple layers of "novels"
break down binary distinctions that readers may have counted on existing, especially those that clearly establish authors of fictions as different
from authors of nonfiction or those that separate an author's life from
his books.

9

A Graveyard for Lunatics
(1990)

A Graveyard for Lunatics (*GL*) is a sequel of sorts to *Death Is a Lonely Business*, set a few years later, in 1954. This novel, like *Death* and *Green Shadows, White Whale*, draws on Bradbury's life, specifically his early work as a screenwriter for Universal Studios. Important characters from *DLB*—Elmo Crumley, Constance Rattigan, and Henry—also appear in *GL* to help the narrator solve the mystery at the heart of the novel.

Patrick Skene Catling, in a review describing Bradbury as "an original romantic with a weird sense of the absurd," categorizes the novel as "comic horror" and a "realistic fantasy" that serves "as the foundation for a ferociously critical satire of the studio system in the 1950s when studio chiefs were almost all-powerful" (Catling 29). Peggy Hecklinger, writing for the *School Library Journal*, praises the way Bradbury creates a "fascinating tour of reality and illusion. . . . Film buffs will revel in the inside atmosphere, and mystery fans will enjoy the complicated kaleidoscopic plot" (135). Reviewer John Kessel praises the strengths of the description of the movie studio and the style of writing, but notes some gaps in how the characters develop and their motivation for actions, which he attributes to Bradbury's preferred style of writing—quickly and without advance planning—and to his "defense of emotion over thought, belief over reality, nostalgia over memory" (Kessel 8).

PLOT DEVELOPMENT

When the novel opens, the narrator and Roy have been working for nearly a month without success to create the "Beast" they need for their movie. On Halloween night, the narrator finds an anonymous note in his office directing him to come to Green Glades Park at midnight to experience a "great revelation. . . . [m]aterial for a best-selling novel or superb screenplay!" (6). Despite his fears, the narrator hires a taxi and goes, only to discover someone apparently climbing out of the cemetery on a ladder. The someone is the body of James Charles Arbuthnot, the former head of the studio who died in an accident twenty years before.

The narrator and the taxi driver flee, leaving behind the body, which had fallen off the ladder. The next day, the narrator meets a famous director, Fritz Wong, and goes to Stage 13 to talk with Roy. Roy's past history of pranks leads the narrator to think that he may have been responsible for the body in the cemetery. Roy has created a Green Town set, reconstructing the house and neighborhood of the narrator's grandparents. The two men sit in the set's porch swing talking, and Roy convinces him that he was not responsible for the plot. Their conversation is interrupted by Manny Leiber, the head of the studio, demanding action on their monster movie.

Later, the narrator and Roy search for the body from the cemetery and find it in the carpenter's shop on the studio lot. They leave it when Manny Leiber arrives with a group of workmen, who also discover the body. Roy receives an anonymous note telling him to come to the Brown Derby restaurant to find the Beast, and he and the narrator go together. At the restaurant, they see a horrendously mutilated man, the perfect Beast. When the man realizes they are looking at him, he tries to leave. They follow him to the Church of St. Sebastian, where they overhear him speaking to a priest, then weeping.

The sight of this mutilated man inspires both men: the narrator to begin writing, Roy to create a model later described by the narrator as "the finest work he had ever done, a proper thing to glide from a far-traveling light-year ship, a hunter of midnight paths across the stars, a dreamer alone behind his terrible, awful, most dreadfully appalling mask" (79). This Beast is a completely accurate recreation of the mutilated man they had seen at the Brown Derby.

Manny responds angrily to the model: he fires Roy and orders him from the studio, and says he will reassign the narrator to a different project. The narrator goes to visit Elmo Crumley, a police detective and friend. While the narrator is celebrating the publication of Elmo's novel with him, he gets a call from Roy, dashes back to the studio, and discovers a scene that he compares to one from Lon Chaney's *The Phantom of the Opera*, which he saw when he was five years old: the shadow of a man who has hung himself. He sees what appears to be Roy's body and, beneath it, the destroyed model of the Beast. At that moment, Doc Phillips comes in with a crew of men, removes Roy's body, and clears out all his personal belongings.

The narrator is determined to discover what is going on inside the studio. The narrator soon comes to believe that Roy is not dead, but hiding out at the studio in disguise. While investigating, the narrator also has to work on the required ending for Fritz Wong's film, a biblical story to which he has been reassigned. The same group of people who are working on the film—Fritz Wong, J. C., Stanislau Groc, and Maggie Botkin—all turn out to have been present twenty years ago when Arbuthnot died. The narrator finally decides to go to Constance Rattigan for help, but at first the former star does not tell him what she knows about the studio's past. A number of mysterious events and more deaths occur.

Persevering, the narrator is able to solve the mystery: he confronts the Beast, who is the horribly mutilated Arbuthnot, and learns how Arbuthnot scripted a coverup, helped by Fritz Wong and others who worked at the studio. Arbuthnot's affair with Emily Sloane was discovered at a Halloween party by her husband, which led to a car chase and an accident. The husband was killed, Emily left mad, and Arbuthnot mutilated. They put out a cover story that everyone died in the accident. Constance took Emily to the sanitarium, and Doc Phillips managed to keep Arbuthnot alive to run his film studio through Manny Leiber. The four who knew about the coverup were Doc, Groc, Manny, and J. C. Fritz and Constance knew some of it, but not that Arbuthnot had survived. The four who knew were paid five thousand dollars a week for life.

What initiated the most recent events at the studio was Doc's discovery that Arbuthnot had cancer. One of the original four conspirators learned about the cancer and started trying to blackmail more money from the studio by means of the "joke" involving the body on the ladder that the narrator found. Arbuthnot, trying to figure out who was acting against him, destroyed Roy's model and miniatures. Roy, wanting revenge, made himself up as the Beast, trapped Arbuthnot, and ran the studio himself.

The narrator finally goes to the Notre Dame set (from *The Hunchback of Notre Dame*, which features the monstrously deformed Quasimodo) and meets Roy on top of the cathedral. Roy takes off the mask and makes his own confession: he arranged his own apparent suicide after finding his work destroyed, made himself up as the Beast, and trapped him. He could then *be* the Beast and run the studio, and he found he loved the power. He released the Beast only when he became horrified to find himself plotting to kill the narrator, his best friend, to maintain his secret and his control of the studio.

At the end, Arbuthnot dies and is truly buried. Manny Leiber is running the studio for real, and although he and the narrator profess continuing hatred for each other, the narrator is willing to write for him in the future. The investigators are all celebrating at the narrator's house when his wife, Peg, returns from her conference to discover a scantily clad Constance biting the narrator's ear.

CHARACTER DEVELOPMENT

The unnamed first-person narrator and protagonist of *Death Is a Lonely Business* is also the main character of this novel, which is set about half a dozen years later. The narrator is in his early thirties and is now married to Peg, who became his fiancée in *DLB*, although during the novel she is away at a conference in Connecticut. He is an atypical character for the hard-boiled mystery genre or even traditional detective fiction: sweet, slightly dumpy, a film fanatic, and a would-be film writer. Unlike traditional male heroes (or even the popular image of the male writer crafted by Ernest Hemingway), the narrator doesn't drink, sleep around, or get into fights. Instead, he chews gum, wears glasses, and falls in love with, marries, and is faithful to his wife, despite the temptation offered by Constance.

This narrator is a grown-up version of the kind of character who was tormented by adolescent peers. In this book, however, he's the writer as well as the protagonist, and is thus able to make himself the hero of the story. Kessel questions the hero's self-portrayal as an "invulnerable" innocent: "This is the novel of a boy dazzled by the movies, whose contact with the harsh realities of their production has left him fundamentally unaffected" (Kessel 8). No matter what seductions or temptations come his way, this protagonist remains true to his values.

The narrator, who used to wait outside the film studio gates as a teenager to collect autographs, has recently made it inside the fence to join his boyhood heroes. He has been hired to write the screenplay for a monster film that his high school friend, Roy Holdstrom, is making the monster for. As noted in Chapter 1, Roy Holdstrom is a character based on Bradbury's friend, special-effects specialist Ray Harryhausen. Roy makes special-effects models of dinosaurs, monsters, and landscapes. The original plan is for the two to create the studio's next major monster movie. On Halloween, mysterious events start taking place at the studio, and the narrator investigates, with the help of his friends from the previous novel: Elmo Crumley, Constance Rattigan, and Henry.

The host of minor but important characters at the film studio include Manny Leiber, the head of the studio; Doc Phillips, a studio doctor; Stanislau Groc, Lenin's make-up man; Fritz Wong, a director; and Maggie Botkin, a film cutter and editor. These characters are part of the studio system. Although the focus of the novel is the making of a film, actors are not particularly represented: only one, J. C. (who believes he is Jesus Christ), the lead actor in one of the studio's films, makes an appearance.

The characters are clearly divided between the business people or managers who run the studio and the creative people who make the films. The two groups of characters are often hostile toward each other because of their different interests. The creative people's disdain for the money people comes through clearly in Maggie's long speech to the narrator, in which she reveals that she has not followed the orders of the studio heads but has saved the original versions of films she's been ordered to cut for financial reasons. The business people and the producers are dedicated to running the studio as a business, and they have more power than the creative people. The creative people, however, have what the narrator sees as the near-magical power of creativity, but they suffer under the control of the owners.

Several characters are part of the mystery plot and are revealed only near the end of the novel: James Charles Arbuthnot (the Beast) and Emily Sloan. Arbuthnot is believed to have been dead for twenty years but is resurrected during the course of the novel. At the start the narrator seems to see his body at the graveyard at the top of a ladder. What is revealed by the Beast, a terrifying yet fascinatingly deformed man, is that he is Arbuthnot, mutilated from the car accident that supposedly caused his death. Emily Sloane, the other survivor of the accident, has been in a comatose condition in a sanitarium for twenty years.

SETTING

The novel opens on October 31, 1954. The setting of *GL* is still Los Angeles, but it is Hollywood rather than the poorer section that Venice was during the time of *DLB*. Specifically, this "tale of two cities" focuses on Maximus film studios and the adjacent Green Glade Park cemetery. These two "cities" are described as the novel opens as different but paired: light/dark, movement/stillness, warmth/cold. The cities are opposites during the day but become one at night. Through the course of the novel, the connections between the two cities are discovered, one of which is a secret underground passage. The studio and the cemetery are two worlds, two linked cities (thus the allusion to Charles Dickens' *A Tale of Two Cities* at the start). By the end of the novel, their connection is made clear; they become one in the course of the novel: "And at long last the two cities were the same" (255). Other important locations are described in terms of their relationship to Maximus and include the Church of St. Sebastian and the Hollyhock House Sanitarium.

Most of the action takes place in the film studio. On the surface, the studio is a workaday world, consisting of studios, offices, stage sets, and a commissary, where the narrator has lunch with various characters. However, because the studio makes movies, the narrator also sees the studio through the eyes of a dreamer and a longtime fan, as a site of enchantment, containing the whole world and more in miniature, consisting of places from all historical periods and imaginary places as well. At the beginning of the novel the narrator likes the studio because it is a place "where everything was clearly defined . . . absolutely sharp beginnings, and ends that were neat and irreversible" (5). Fascinated by the movie sets, the narrator describes the "world" of the studio: "And the night watchman was the only motion prowling along from India to France to prairie Kansas to brownstone New York to Piccadilly to the Spanish Steps, covering twenty thousand miles of territorial incredibility in twenty brief moments" (4). The narrator loves to walk at night, when the studio takes on its most magical aspect: "chariots rushing by in the air, or sand blowing across Beau Geste's ghost-haunted desert . . . Champs-Elysees . . . Niagara . . . Indianapolis . . . Caesar's wounds . . . Churchill . . . a long-after-midnight collision of buried voices and lost musics caught in a time cloud between buildings" (154–55).

THEMES

A Graveyard for Lunatics is similar to *Death Is a Lonely Business* in its mystery plot, but even more than the first novel, *GL* brings conventions from other genres to bear on its theme of how the inevitability of death and the persistent human belief that something will live on after physical death leads to a fascination with stories about death and resurrection. Conventions from horror films, specifically *The Phantom of the Opera* (apparently one of Bradbury's favorite films), and passion plays create a sense that there is more to the novel than simply "solving" the question of what happened twenty years ago.

Passion plays are dramas that deal with the important events of Jesus Christ's life: specifically, his trial, crucifixion, and resurrection. In *GL*, the traditional clues expected of a mystery do not exist, or play little importance. More important are the stories (repeatedly presented as confessions, both to the priest at St. Sebastian and to the narrator) that the narrator must gather from other characters.

Although the distance between a horror movie (such as *The Hunchback of Notre Dame* or *The Phantom of the Opera*) and a dramatic retelling of Christ's death and resurrection may seem immense, both stories focus on an ever-present question for humanity: what happens after the death of the physical body? Horror stories deal with death and spirits living on afterward in a very different manner than passion plays, but the basic events are similar in outline. Both plot structures share the basic elements of a character dying, perhaps going to an underworld (metaphorical or literal, symbolized by catacombs or hidden cellar passageways), and then coming back to life.

The horror elements are evoked by the narrator, who remembers being terribly scared by *Phantom of the Opera*, especially the scene with the shadow of the hanging body of a stagehand. The existence of the secret passage and a mutilated Beast also recall traditional horror conventions. Other generic horror elements include the mysterious note, a graveyard at midnight, and the presence of multiple bodies that disappear and reappear. When the narrator, Henry, and Elmo Crumley go into Arbuthnot's empty vault and Crumley orders the narrator to shut the door, the narrator objects, citing the horror films he's seen. And, right on cue, after Crumley shoves the door nearly shut, someone from the outside swings it shut and locks them in.

The passion play elements occur in the religious imagery and biblical references, including the repeated references to the Stations of the Cross, and from specific plot elements related to the film the narrator is assigned to after Manny fires Roy. This film is about the life of Christ, and the narrator is assigned to write the ending. He keeps asking the studio people whether or not they've ever read the Bible, and is inspired by the Bible in his creation of an "ending." Other religious elements include J. C., a former studio carpenter who was cast as Christ in films and who now believes himself to be Jesus Christ, and who has a habit of spending time on a cross.

ALTERNATIVE PERSPECTIVE: A SEMIOTIC READING

Semiotic theory is based on theories about how languages work developed initially by the linguist Ferdinand de Saussure and added to by many subsequent theorists, including Umberto Eco. Saussure developed a theory that words are not just labels for things. Instead, language is a code that relies on complex relationships between linguistic elements. Words do not exist in isolation: their meaning depends on other words. Examples of the relational aspect of words are: man/woman and day/ night (Barry 42). The meanings of these words depend on their being part of a system; in the case of these terms, the relationship is a binary (and oppositional) one. The meanings of words are arbitrary and constructed by humans, not essentially contained within what is named. Eco argues that the relationship between words (or "signs") and their meanings is always dynamic and multiple, which means there can be "slippage" and networks of associations.

Thinking of the extent to which the "meaning" of words can be understood in light of semiotic theory leads to the awareness that a word, image, or symbol can carry multiple meanings. Two "signs" are important to the structure of the novel as a whole: "Christ" and "the Beast."

The multiple meanings assigned to Christ, or the multiple representations of Christ, are the film script (about Jesus Christ); the Bible, which is quoted directly by J. C. and which inspires the narrator to create the ending for the film; and J. C., who has a driver's license with the name Jesus Christ on it. Additionally, the narrator compares himself to Christ in a metaphor at the start of the novel: "Here were also the Stations of the Cross and a trail of ever-replenished blood as screenwriters groaned by to Calvary carrying a backbreaking load of revisions, pursued by directors with scourges and film cutters with razor sharp knives" (4). In this passage, the narrator, who is a screenwriter, compares writers to Christ by referring to the Stations of the Cross, depictions of Jesus' travails as he carried the cross to his place of crucifixion. In this comparison, directors and film cutters are compared to the soldiers and others who persecuted Christ. The studio has built a representation of Calvary (the hill where Jesus was crucified) as a set, and J. C. often hides there, resting on a cross, where he eventually dies.

"The Beast" is a sign that also contains multiple meanings. Roy's models, monsters or dinosaurs on miniature landscapes, are filmed as representing imaginary or extinct monsters from other planets or from Earth's past. Repeated references to Lon Chaney's character of Quasimodo evoke the idea of "human" as "monster." Arbuthnot/the Beast is both a man mutilated by an accident and a more-than-human or other-than-human creature. Roy melds the several possible meanings by making himself up as the Beast, filming himself live, and then facing the Beast as a "mirror representation" to defeat him. The two "signs," both carrying multiple meanings, slip into each other, one becoming the other.

10

Green Shadows, White Whale
(1992)

Green Shadows, White Whale (*GSWW*) describes the time Ray Bradbury spent in Ireland in 1953 writing the screenplay for the film *Moby Dick*, directed by John Huston. This novel, like *Death Is a Lonely Business* and *A Graveyard for Lunatics*, is one of Bradbury's semiautobiographical novels, although *GSWW* dispenses with the conventions of murder mysteries and horror films. Instead, the writing process becomes a major focus of the book along with the narrator's desire to learn more about Ireland.

Francis King, reviewing the novel in *Spectator*, notes the "mixture of fact and fantasy" in the novel, observing that "most of the fact is about Huston and the film, most of the fantasy about an Ireland which for Bradbury often seems to be as mythical as the white whale" (King 30). The relationship between the autobiographical sections and the fantasy sections is complex. King also notes the problem with the level of stereotyping of the Irish characters that other critics have noted as well.

Bruce Cook, an Irish critic writing in *Catholic World*, in "Ray Bradbury and the Irish," discusses Bradbury's handling of Irish characters in several short stories and plays, a number of which are included in the novel. According to Cook, "the greatest temptation for a writer in dealing with the Irish is to be taken in by their quaintness" (225). Even Irish writers have to take care in this regard, and Cook notes problems with the stereotypical characters and stock situations in Bradbury's short pieces.

Other critics have generally praised the comedy, exaggeration, and

pace of this novel, which covers approximately a year in the life of Bradbury, including seven months spent in Ireland working with John Huston.

PLOT DEVELOPMENT

The structure of the novel is episodic, consisting of thirty-three numbered chapters, several of which were published as short stories. The
narrator has two major goals, which he declares to an Irish customs
inspector in the first chapter. The first is to conquer *Moby Dick*, the im-
posing novel by Herman Melville, by crafting a screenplay of it for John
Huston, one of the narrator's greatest heroes. The second is to study the
Irish. The narrator freely admits to being prejudiced about the Irish, since
he spent his youth being beaten up by Irish kids or beating them up in
his turn. These two purposes, or quests, shape the plot structure of the
novel.

On his first afternoon in Ireland he goes for a cab ride, but ends up
on a bicycle when the car breaks down. As he's riding he meets a man
named Mike, who takes him to Heeber Finn's pub to help him in his
project of studying Ireland. While they are drinking, an accident outside
catches their attention. A short story, "The Great Collision of Monday
Last," is the basis for the following chapter. It relates how a man staggers
into the pub with dramatic news about a collision, which (to the "Yank's"
great surprise) turns out to be an accident involving two men on bicycles.
A doctor and a priest are called in, and a great deal of excitement takes
place—to the consternation of the narrator, who keeps expecting such a
dramatic accident to involve cars.

The writer, late because of his detour to the pub, then has his first
meeting with John Huston. The narrator feels worshipful toward the
great director, and plans a future working for this genius. A disagreeable
scene soon follows in which the director attacks his wife for refusing to
help smuggle someone out of Spain. He accuses her of being "yellow,"
an insult that he will often hurl at the narrator over the next few months.
The narrator responds to this scene with sympathy for Ricki. He also
remembers a warning he received before leaving Beverly Hills from the
wife of a former screenwriter, who advised him not to go because the
director is so monstrous.

Throughout the book, the two structures—the quest for Ireland and
the quest for the White Whale—intertwine. Additionally, the plot dealing

with the quest for the White Whale mixes with the conflict with John Huston—the Beast—with the narrator comparing himself to the captain Ahab: the narrator is the "pursuer of the Whale. I was a small ahab, with no capital up front," but the "Whiteness outpaced my poor strokes and my inadequate boat" (68).

Fifteen chapters focus on the narrator's search for Ireland, usually inside Heeber Finn's pub or a Dublin pub that is open on Sundays, the Four Provinces. A great part of his search for Ireland is satisfied by stories that Heeber tells him. The first story is what happened in Kilcock during the Easter Uprising on 1916, a failed attempt to achieve Irish independence that led to the execution of fourteen men in Dublin. In Kilcock, according to Heeber, the fathers of the pub regulars decided to burn down the house of Lord Kilgotten, but forgot to take along matches. The Lord invited them in, offered refreshments, and talked them first into putting off their plans until the next evening because it would be more convenient, and then into helping him save his art works. The men agree, but when they run into problems getting the art home or into their houses, they return them to the lord and go peacefully home.

Heeber's second story is about the time the Dublin College of Surgeons got drunk and sent a cable inviting the American Medical Association to Dublin. The Americans made an unfavorable report about Dublin hospitals and were thrown out of Ireland and ignored. His third story is about the time George Bernard Shaw, a famous playwright, got lost and ended up at Heeber's pub with a flat tire. Shaw, a teetotaler and the author of scandalous plays, engaged in a philosophical debate about the nature of the Irish and the existence of God with the local priest, Father O'Malley.

The narrator also learns about Ireland by accompanying Mike on a "wild night out." The narrator wonders if "beneath the rain-drenched sod, the flinty rock . . . was there one small seed of fire which, fanned, might break volcanoes free and boil the rains to steam? Was there then somewhere a Baghdad harem . . . the absolute perfect tint of woman unadorned?" (30). However, the wild night out consists of dog races, where he wins a couple of shillings, and ends by ten o'clock.

One aspect of Ireland that gives the narrator particular trouble is Dublin's beggars, described in chapter 13, originally published as a short story, "The Beggar on O'Connell Bridge," and chapter 23, originally published as the short story "McGillahee's Brat." The narrator sees numerous beggars in Dublin and is never able to resist giving them money, with the exception of one man who stands on O'Connell Bridge without a hat. The narrator is at first angry with the man, feeling that he is faking his blindness, and then tries to make amends for never giving him money by buying him a cap. Unfortunately, the man commits suicide by jumping from the bridge before the narrator arrives with the gift.

The second beggar story is less grim and more fantastic: the narrator, while giving money to a beggar woman with a baby, recognizes them as beggars he had seen on his earlier trip to Ireland in 1939. They try to escape him, but he searches for them for days until he finds them in the Four Provinces, drinking. He finally convinces them that he is not a threat, and hears the "Brat's" story: he is not a baby, or rather, he has remained the size of a baby for forty years. Born into a family of beggars, he never grew up; his parents died, and the woman he now begs with is his sister. But they have saved nearly enough money to emigrate to New York.

The narrator also learns about Ireland by directly experiencing life there, primarily from living in a hotel. When John persuades his friend Tom Hurley to come to Ireland with his fiancée Lisa Helm for a Hunt Wedding, the narrator is drafted to help do a great deal of the work, including finding a Protestant minister in the Catholic part of Ireland who is willing to marry two adults who openly admit they have been living in sin.

In chapter 15, originally published as "The Haunting of the New," the narrator gets a call at three in the morning call from Nora, an old friend whom he met on his first trip to Ireland. A member of the wealthy elite in Ireland, Nora inherited a house, Grynwood, and has lived a lavish life of parties and debauchery ever since. When her house burned down four years ago, she went to great lengths to rebuild it exactly as it was. However, in one of the more fantastic elements in the novel, this new, "innocent" house has rejected her, and all her friends, as sinful. She thinks she can give it to the narrator, but the house rejects him as well.

Alcohol plays a major part in the narrator's quest for Ireland, which occurs mostly in pubs. In chapter 22, originally published as "The First Day of Lent," the narrator learns that his friend Mike drives smoothly and slowly only when drunk. When Mike gives up alcohol for Lent, he turns into a demon driver who terrifies the narrator so much that he brings him a bottle of whiskey and begs him to give something else up for Lent. The narrator happens to be in the pub when the news comes that Lord Kilgotten has died and left a secret codicil specifying that his wine collection be poured over his coffin. Deciding that the will does not specify how the wine moves from bottle to grave, the men (including the narrator) end up standing around the grave drinking the wine.

Most of the encounters with the Irish involve men. The only two Irish women are the beggar girl (in chapter 23, where the main focus is on the Brat) and an old woman who plays the harp on the streets. In this encounter, the narrator is depressed one Sunday afternoon in Dublin. He goes to the Four Provinces in the afternoon and meets an old man who is drinking and complaining about how people are never grateful for all the wonders of life. The narrator leaves in a bad mood, then hears harp music, played by an old woman on the street. He praises her playing and tells her how it has helped him. Imagine, he says, being lonely and stuck in a hotel, then you "turn a corner, and there's this little woman with a golden harp and everything she plays is another season—autumn, spring, summer . . . a free-for-all. And the ice melts, the fog lifts, the wind burns with June, and ten years shuck off your life" (151). His praise angers her, and she cannot play because he's spoiled it all. He goes around a corner and waits because he hears her trying to play. She regains her music, then he sneaks by, her eyes are shut and her hands were "moving . . . like the fresh hands of a very young girl who has first known rain and washes her palms in its clear waterfalls" (153). He realizes the only way to thank her is to go back to his own creative work and do it as well as he can.

This event, with its focus on the work of creating art, whether music or writing, connects the quest for Ireland to the quest for the White Whale, which also involves the conflict with John Huston. This second quest is the focus of thirteen chapters. At the beginning of the novel, the writer is elated to be in Ireland with one of his greatest heroes. The first chapters do not focus on writing the screenplay: rather, the writer works alone in his room and spends time with Huston, engaging in his social activities or masculine rituals. One afternoon, Huston tries to start his own bullfight as they are crossing a field. Later he encourages the writer to take up foxhunting, requiring the purchase of riding clothes and riding lessons.

In chapter 8, Huston plays the hypnotist and puts the reluctant writer under, eliciting the "subconscious" message from the writer to himself to write the "greatest, most wonderful, finest screenplay in the history of the world" (35). The narrator also has to spend a great deal of time working on the Hunt Wedding. By chapter 11, the writer has begun to have problems with his writing, and his conflicts with Huston intensify.

By chapter 16, the narrator is hiding out from the director, not wanting to continue riding lessons. When he finally confronts Huston, it's to give him a choice: getting the screenplay or having his writer learn to ride for a foxhunt. Huston immediately backs down. Successful confrontations with Huston occur throughout the rest of the novel.

A major conflict occurs in chapter 24 when the narrator receives a cable announcing that he has won a national literary award and five thousand dollars. Rushing out to tell Huston about it, the narrator finds himself challenged by both Huston and his friend Jake, who jeer at his plans to spend the money on a house for his family, demand that he invest it, and then suddenly start to theorize about how men are attracted to other men. The two men each relate stories of homoerotic attractions from their youth (their own or their friends'), then challenge the narrator to tell his secret. The narrator strikes back by telling them that he never felt any attraction to males in the past, but that he's in love with Huston now, and that he will knock on Jake's door later that night. The two men deflect the narrator's challenge to their masculinity by threatening to bet all his prize money on a horse, then argue about the narrator's cowardice over money. He admits he's a coward, but then says he will bet all his money on Oscar Wilde (an Anglo-Irish playwright jailed for homosexuality).

The next conflict comes when Huston jokingly tells reporters they are lunching with that the narrator doesn't really care about the screenplay. The narrator confronts him about the accusation, only to be told it was a joke. He gets his revenge by writing a short horror story in which a director named John plays practical jokes on a writer. The writer meets a banshee, the spirit of a woman who returns to confront her betrayer, a womanizing man. By the end of the story, the writer has sent John out to meet the banshee and, probably, to his death as well.

In the novel, the narrator gives the story to Huston to read, prompting the latter to swear off practical jokes. The final conflict, ending with the narrator winning decisively, comes after he tries to hypnotize Huston. The narrator wins this competition by completing the screenplay in a seven-hour bout of inspired writing. As a result, Huston gives up on his plan to force him to fly to London (the narrator is terrified of flying) and begins to speak to him again. In a sense, the novel can be read as a complex extension of the banshee story—a story of a conflict the writer wins.

CHARACTER DEVELOPMENT

The major character in the novel is the narrator, who arrives in Ireland with his typewriter and minimal luggage. While the character is based on Bradbury at the time he wrote the screenplay for *Moby Dick*, a comparison of the narrator's situation as described in the novel and the information available in Nolan's biographical profile make it clear that Bradbury has felt free to fictionalize for the purpose of the story. Bradbury took his wife and daughters to Ireland in September 1953, and they stayed through April (Nolan 60). The narrator in *GSWW* does have a wife and family, mentioned at key points, but a great deal of the book's narrative power comes from the fact that he is alone in Ireland, his family left across the ocean.

As with the narrators of the earlier two novels, the narrator's name is never given: his friends and acquaintances refer to him variously as "Yank" (Heeber Finn and the regulars at the pub), or "H. G." (John Huston's nickname for him, from science fiction pioneer H. G. Wells), or "Willy" (his friend Nora's nickname for him, from William Shakespeare). The issue of what people call the narrator is handled differently in this novel than in the earlier two; in the first two novels, the narrator did not seem to bear any grudges toward the friends who called him "the Crazy" or referred to him by the names of well-known science fiction writers. In this novel, however, when news comes that he has won a literary prize along with a five thousand-dollar cash prize, he is elated: "for years people have called me Buck Rogers or Flash Gordon. . . . But now, maybe someone will call me by my right name" (174). When he goes to tell his friends the news, however, Huston's response is to call him by anything but his right name: "Son of Jules Verne," "Flash Gordon's Bastard Brother," and "kid" (175–77) are all used rapidly, in an apparent attempt to diminish the writer's stature.

The narrator, although married and with a family, presents himself as naive, even innocent, compared to the worldly and sophisticated Hollywood director John Huston and his circle of friends, who include both Hollywood stars and the Anglo-Irish elite who participate in fox hunts. Huston and his wife Ricki live in Courtdown House, outside Dublin, regularly travel around Europe, host friends from America, and generally live a glamorous "Hollywood" lifestyle. For a time, the narrator tries to participate in that lifestyle, togging himself out in hunting dress and taking riding lessons, but he also spends a good deal of time in the village of Kilcock at a pub owned by Heeber Finn, where he gets to know the Irishmen who are poor or working class.

A good deal of the conflict in the novel comes from the relationship between the narrator and Huston, whom he describes at times as a hero and friend and other times as a monster and beast. The love-hate relationship between the writer and the director, a young man and an older man, characterizes their relationship throughout the novel. As a character, Huston is drawn as larger than life, energetic, prone to involved practical jokes and temper tantrums, competitive, and given to strong enthusiasms. He takes an ordinary call from a friend and, within a few minutes, convinces him to fly to Ireland with his fiancée for a "Hunt Wedding." The young writer seems to be a particularly apt victim for Huston's pranks, and, from the start, finds himself sympathizing with the director's wife.

Other important characters are the regulars at Heeber Finn's pub: Heeber Finn, the pub owner; O'Gavin, a poacher; Casey, a blacksmith and automobile mechanic; Kelly, a turf accountant or bookie; Timulty, described as an art connoisseur from seeing stamps in the post office where he works; Carmichael, who runs the telephone exchange; and Mike, who drives the narrator not only on his trips between the hotel in Dublin and Courtdown House but also on his journeys to "discover" Ireland. The narrator meets Mike the first day, and Mike is the one who introduces him to Heeber's pub.

Besides these characters, who appear at regular intervals throughout the book, other characters include the beggars of Ireland, featured in two sections, and characters from the past, who figure in the stories told at the pub: the local lord, George Bernard Shaw (featured in a story about Heeber's pub), and a group of exotic "aliens" (gay men) who travel to Ireland just for the day to see winter. The title of the novel also establishes two nonhuman characters: Ireland and the White Whale. Ireland and the Whale as the object of the writer's quest inhabit the writer's imagination throughout the course of the novel.

THEMES

The theme of *Green Shadows, White Whale* is the creation of identity, of maturing, through the process of writing. At the beginning of the novel, the narrator is technically an adult (married, with children), but he sees himself as a young man on a quest to solve several important problems in his life. Spending time with an older, more experienced man, his great hero, the young man moves rapidly from hero worship to conflict and back again. The narrator literally writes himself into the story he is writing, and in conquering the novel *Moby Dick*, the narrator is also able to conquer John Huston, the Beast of his fears.

The screenplay the narrator is writing is both the basis for a major conflict with Huston and the means by which the narrator wins this conflict. Along the way, a short story the narrator writes (that is, one of Bradbury's stories) wins him a point in the ongoing conflict. Finally, the novel is the next level of writing about the process of writing as creation: Bradbury re/creates his younger self and sees him to a new level of maturity. This most recent of Bradbury's autobiographical fantasies show the narrator growing beyond the children or adolescents depicted in the earlier novels, and *Green Shadows* ends with a narrator who has apparently achieved a stronger sense of maturity and self through the process of writing. The overwhelming impression of these autobiographical novels is of a writer's mind, a mind that does not experience events as fully realized until they are recollected and (re)written.

ALTERNATIVE PERSPECTIVE: A QUEER READING

Lesbian and gay theory is a relatively new area of literary criticism and is related to feminist theory in several important ways. The first way is that sexual orientation, like gender, is the central focus of analysis; second, gay and lesbian theory also has political goals (Barry 140). One specific subcategory of gay and lesbian theory that has grown in the 1990s is "queer theory," which has appropriated an insulting term in order to redefine it. Queer theory focuses on identifying the "political and social interests" that lesbians may share more with gay men than with heterosexual feminists (Barry 141).

Constructing a queer reading is based on the assumption that heterosexuality is not "normal" or superior to homosexuality. Sexual identity is not stable or universal; categories like "gay" or "straight" are constructed and can act as oppressive or liberatory. Like feminist criticism, queer theory can serve as a means of analyzing texts; it is not a statement about writers, readers, or critics.

Green Shadows, White Whale has several sections in which Bradbury deals openly with homosocial and homosexual issues. "Homosocial" is a term that means all-male social environments from which women are excluded. The first section is the description of Tom Hurley, who comes to Ireland to get married. The narrator describes him as the perfect example of a man: "He was everything men would like to be if they were honest with themselves, everything John wanted to be and couldn't quite live up to, and a hopeless and crazily reckless idea for someone like me to admire from a distance, having been born and bred of reluctance, second thoughts, premonitions, depressions, and lack of will" (41). Masculinity is figured as involving travel and independence, physical fitness from multiple sports and activities, physical beauty, and a "fire" that cannot be damped by age, other men, or women: "Tom was his own mount and saddle, he rode himself and did so with masculine beauty" (41). Not even John, the writer's great hero, quite lives up to this standard.

The second example is the conflict the narrator has with Huston and Jake after receiving notification of his literary award and prize money. In response to the news that he plans to spend his money on furniture, bookcases, and golf clubs for his father, the older, more sophisticated men react with horror. They offer to invest his prize money for him, but when he resists, the conversation suddenly changes. Huston asks what he reads, then interrupts the list to ask if he had read Havelock Ellis and the Kinsey Report. In a three-page conversation, Huston and Jake gang up on the narrator, discussing not only the general theory of homosexuality and the concept of men falling in love with male heroes, but telling specific stories about themselves. Huston and Jake tell stories, but the narrator says he never felt anything for men, then "wins" the contest by telling them that he's really in love with them.

The third example is chapter 28 (originally published as "The Cold Wind and the Warm"), in which a group of rich American tourists, all men, come to Ireland to see winter. These exotic aliens are described as willowy, as a "corps de ballet" and "six hothouse roses." In the story, the regulars from Heeber Finn's pub study the group, with one of them eventually arguing for the similarities between the Irish and the gay men (to some disagreement at first). The two groups, he notes, share similar interests: both like poetry and songs, writing and dancing, and drink; they marry late in life, if ever, and avoid women; and most importantly, both primarily spend time with groups of other men.

The comparisons between the Irish and gay men (which the narrator admits could be dangerous to make) can best be understood as focusing on "homosocial" (single-sex social) grouping rather than any overt sexual practice. The regulars at Heeber's pub—all male—see another all-male group, and several characters point out the similarities.

The narrator, in contrast, seems to align himself with women, although (given his wife's absence) this alignment is not primarily sexual in nature. His sympathy for Ricki leads to their alliance over each having to bear the brunt of her husband's anger and often hostile "jokes," especially his repeated accusations that Ricki or the narrator are "yellow." His friendship with Nora, which may have been more romantic or sexual in the past but has now mutated to friendship, is shown to be completely nonsexual when they sleep together like frightened children. The final conflict with Huston is described by the narrator as being like a marital quarrel: When the director stops speaking to him for days after the hypnosis, the narrator says that "I was the rejected lover, the forever-to-be-forgotten and never-forgiven wife. The wonderful marriage had turned sour" (260). The "marriage" and lovers' quarrel here are metaphorical, but the professional relationship between two adult men is cast in language symbolic of a sexual relationship.

A queer reading of *GSWW* focuses attention on the extent to which some groups, including women and gay men, are marginalized in a patriarchal culture. Queer theory leads to speculation on the extent to which oppressed groups might share characteristics not valued by the dominant culture: the Irish in relation to the English are thus similar to gay men's relationship to the dominant heterosexual society.

In his interactions with other characters, the narrator perceives himself as an outsider: a writer who tends to look on or observe, but also a person set apart by differences. He is not Irish, not a worldly Hollywood sophisticate, nor a powerful, authoritative man. Occupying a position of less power in his relationship with Huston may be one indication of why the writer-narrator fits in much better with the Catholic, working-class Irish men at Heeber Finn's pub than with the wealthy, elite Anglo-Irish and the Hollywood sophisticates.

Bibliography

WORKS BY RAY BRADBURY

Fiction

Novels

Dandelion Wine. Garden City, New York: Doubleday, 1957.

Death is a Lonely Business. New York: Knopf, 1985.

Fahrenheit 451. New York: Ballantine, 1953.

A Graveyard for Lunatics. New York: Knopf, 1994.

Green Shadows, White Whale. New York: Knopf, 1992.

The Halloween Tree. New York: Knopf, 1972. (Juvenile.)

The Illustrated Man. Garden City, New York: Doubleday, 1951.

The Martian Chronicles. Garden City, New York: Doubleday, 1950.

The Novels of Ray Bradbury. Toronto: Granada, 1984. (Contains *Dandelion Wine, Fahrenheit 451,* and *Something Wicked This Way Comes.*)

Ray Bradbury. New York: Heinemann, 1987. (Contains complete *Dandelion Wine, Fahrenheit 451, The Golden Apples of the Sun, The Illustrated Man,* and *The Martian Chronicles.*)

The Silver Locusts. London: Rupert Hart-Davis, 1951. (First British edition of *The Martian Chronicles;* contents vary from U.S. and other British editions.)

Something Wicked This Way Comes. New York: Simon & Schuster, 1962.

Story Collections

Classic Stories I. New York: Bantam, 1990. (Includes selections from *The Golden Apples of the Sun* and *R Is for Rocket*.)
Classic Stories II. New York: Bantam, 1990. (Includes selections from *A Medicine for Melancholy*, and *S Is for Space*.)
Dark Carnival. Sauk City, Wis.: Arkham, 1947. (Story Collection.)
Dinosaur Tales. New York: Bantam, 1983. (Juvenile.)
Driving Blind. New York: Avon, 1997.
The Golden Apples of the Sun. Garden City, N.Y.: Doubleday, 1953.
I Sing the Body Electric! New York: Knopf, 1969.
Long after Midnight. New York: Knopf, 1976.
The Machineries of Joy. New York: Simon & Schuster, 1964.
A Medicine for Melancholy. Garden City, N.Y.: Doubleday, 1959.
The October Country. New York: Ballantine, 1955.
Quicker Than the Eye. New York: Avon, 1996.
Ray Bradbury. London: Harrap, 1975.
R Is for Rocket. Garden City, N.Y.: Doubleday, 1961.
The Small Assassin. London: Ace, 1962. (Selections from *Dark Carnival* and *The October Country*.)
S Is for Space. Garden City, N.Y.: Doubleday, 1966.
The Stories of Ray Bradbury. New York: Knopf, 1980.
The Toynbee Convector. New York: Knopf, 1988.
To Sing Strange Songs. Exeter, U.K.: Wheaton, 1979.
Twice 22. Garden City, N.Y.: Doubleday, 1966. (Includes *The Golden Apples of the Sun* and *A Medicine for Melancholy*.)
The Vintage Bradbury. New York: Vintage, 1965.

Drama

The Anthem Sprinters and Other Antics. New York: Dial, 1963.
The Pedestrian. New York: Samuel French, 1966.
Pillar of Fire and Other Plays. New York: Bantam, 1975.
The Wonderful Ice Cream Suit and Other Plays. New York: Bantam, 1972.

Poetry

The Complete Poems of Ray Bradbury. New York: Ballantine, 1982. (Includes poems from three earlier volumes.)
The Haunted Computer and the Android Pope. New York: Knopf, 1981.
When Elephants Last in the Dooryard Bloomed. New York: Knopf, 1973.
Where Robot Mice and Robot Men Run Round in Robot Towns. New York: Knopf,

1977.

Anthologies Edited by Bradbury

The Circus of Dr. Lao and Other Improbable Stories. New York: Bantam, 1956.
Timeless Stories for Today and Tomorrow. New York: Bantam, 1952.

Nonfiction

Zen in the Art of Writing. New York: Bantam, 1992.

WORKS ABOUT RAY BRADBURY

Biographies

Nolan, William F. *The Ray Bradbury Companion.* Detroit: Gale Research, 1975.
Wolfe, Gary K. "Bradbury." *The Dictionary of Literary Biography,* vol. 8. Detroit: Gale Research, 1981.

General Information

Abrams, Kathleen S. "Literature and Science: An Interdisciplinary Approach to Environmental Studies." *Curriculum Review* 18, no. 4 (October 1979): 302–4.
Burleson, Donald R. "Connings: Bradbury/Oates." *Studies in Weird Fiction* 11 (1992): 24–29.
Dominianni, Robert. "Ray Bradbury's 2026: A Year with Current Value." *English Journal* 73, no. 7 (1984): 49–51.
Eller, Jonathan. "Bradbury Bio & Biblio." Email to Robin Reid. 8 November 1999.
Greenberg, Martin Harry and Joseph D. Olander, eds. *Ray Bradbury.* New York: Taplinger, 1980. (Many individual essays are cited separately in this bibliography.)
Johnson, Wayne L. "The Invasion Stories of Ray Bradbury." In *Critical Encounters: Writers and Themes in Science Fiction,* edited by Dick Riley, 23–40. New York: Ungar, 1978.
———. *Ray Bradbury.* New York: Frederick Ungar, 1980.
Johnston, Richard, and Chris Jepson. *The Ray Bradbury Page.* 2 November 1998. <http://www.brookingsbookcom/bradbury/bradbury.html>
Kagle, Steven E. "Homage to Melville: Ray Bradbury and the Nineteenth-Century American Romance." In *The Celebration of the Fantastic: Selected Papers from the Tenth Anniversary International Conference on the Fantastic in the Arts,* edited by Donald E. Morse, 279–89, Marshall B. Tymn, and Csilla Bertha, Contributions to the Study of Science Fiction and Fantasy, No. 49. Westport, Conn.: Greenwood, 1992.
Linkfield, Thomas P. "The Fiction of Ray Bradbury: Universal Themes in Midwestern Settings." *Midwestern Miscellany* 8 (1980): 94–101.

Logsdon, Loren. "Ray Bradbury's 'The Kilimanjaro Device': The Need to Correct the Errors of Time." *Midwestern Miscellany* 20 (1992): 28–39.

McNelly, Willis E. "Ray Bradbury, 1920–." In *Science Fiction Writers: Critical Studies of the Major Authors from the Early Nineteenth Century to the Present Day*, edited by Everett Franklin Bleiler, 171–78. New York: Scribner's, 1982.

———. "Ray Bradbury: Past, Present, and Future." In *Voices for the Future: Essays on Major Science Fiction Writers*, edited by Thomas D. Clareson, 167–75. Bowling Green, Ohio: Bowling Green University Popular Press, 1976.

McNurlin, Kathleen Woitel. "A Question of Ethics: Themes in the Science Fiction Genre." *Interdisciplinary Humanities* 12, no. 4 (1995): 19–36.

Miller, Calvin. "Ray Bradbury: Hope in a Doubtful Age." In *Reality and the Vision*, edited by Philip Yancey, 92–101. Dallas: Word, 1990.

Mogen, David. *Ray Bradbury*. Twayne's United States Authors Series. Boston: Twayne. 1986.

Patrouch, Joe. "Symbolic Settings in Science Fiction: H. G. Wells, Ray Bradbury, and Harlan Ellison." *Journal of the Fantastic in the Arts* 1, no. 3 (1988): 37–45.

Pell, Sarah-Warner J. "Style Is the Man: Imagery in Bradbury's Fiction." In *Ray Bradbury*, edited by Martin Harry Greenberg and Joseph D. Olander, 186–94. New York: Taplinger, 1980.

Pierce, Hazel. "Ray Bradbury and the Gothic Tradition." In *Ray Bradbury*, edited by Martin Harry Greenberg and Joseph D. Olander, 165–85. New York: Taplinger, 1980.

Slusser, George Edgar. *The Bradbury Chronicles*. Popular Writers of Today series. San Bernardino, Calif.: Borgo, 1977.

Spencer, Susan. "The Post-Apocalyptic Library: Oral and Literate Culture in *Fahrenheit 451* and *A Canticle for Leibowitz*." *Extrapolation* 32, no. 4 (1991): 331–42.

Stockwell, Peter. "Language, Knowledge, and the Stylistics of Science Fiction." In *Subjectivity and Literature from the Romantics to the Present Day*, edited by Philip Shaw and Peter Stockwell, 101–12. London: Pinter, 1991.

Stupple, A. James. "The Past, the Future, and Ray Bradbury." In *Ray Bradbury*, edited by Martin Harry Greenberg and Joseph D. Olander, 24–32. New York: Taplinger, 1980.

Sullivan, Anita T. "Ray Bradbury and Fantasy." *English Journal* 61 (1972): 1309–14.

Teicher, Morton I. "Ray Bradbury and Thomas Wolfe: Fantasy and the Fantastic." *Thomas Wolfe Review* 12, no. 3. (Fall 1998): 17–19.

Touponce, William F. "The Existential Fabulous: A Reading of Ray Bradbury's 'The Golden Apples of the Sun'." *Mosaic: A Journal for the Interdisciplinary Study of Literature* 13, nos. 3–4 (1980): 203–18.

———. *Ray Bradbury and the Poetics of Reverie*. 2nd ed. San Bernadino, Calif.: Borgo Press, 1998.

Wood, Diane S. "Bradbury and Atwood: Exile as Rational Decision." In *The Literature of Emigration and Exile*, edited by James Whitlark and Wendell Aycock, 131–42. Studies in Comparative Literature Series. Lubbock, Tex.: Texas Tech University Press, 1992.

Bibliography

Eller, Jon R. "The Stories of Ray Bradbury: An Annotated Finding List." *Bulletin of Bibliography* 49, no. 1 (March 1992): 27–51.

REVIEWS AND CRITICISM

The Martian Chronicles

Eller, Jonathan. "The Body Eclectic: Sources of Ray Bradbury's *Martian Chronicles.*" *University of Mississippi Studies in English* 11–12 (1993): 376–410.

Gallagher, Edward J. "The Thematic Structure of 'The Martian Chronicles.' " In *Ray Bradbury*, edited by Martin Harry Greenberg and Joseph D. Olander, 55–82. New York: Taplinger, 1980.

Hoskinson, Kevin. "*The Martian Chronicles* and *Fahrenheit 451*: Ray Bradbury's Cold War Novels." *Extrapolation* 36, no. 4 (1995): 345–59.

Menefee, Christine C. "Imagining Mars: The New Chronicles." *School Library Journal* (December 1994): 38–39.

Pratt, Fletcher. "Beyond Stars, Atoms & Hell." Review of *The Martian Chronicles*. *Saturday Review of Literature*, 17 June 1950, 32.

Prosser, H. L. "Teaching Sociology with *The Martian Chronicles*." *Social Education* 47 (March 1983): 212–15, 221.

Rabkin, Eric S. "To Fairyland by Rocket: Bradbury's *The Martian Chronicles*." In *Ray Bradbury*, edited by Martin Harry Greenberg and Joseph D. Olander, 110–26. New York: Taplinger, 1980.

Sandow, Gregory. "So Long, Pittsburgh." *Village Voice*, 15 June 1982, 13–14.

Valis, Noel M. "*The Martian Chronicles* and Jorge Luis Borges." *Extrapolation* 20 (1979): 50–59.

Wolfe, Gary K. "The Frontier Myth in Ray Bradbury." In *Ray Bradbury*, edited by Martin Harry Greenberg and Joseph D. Olander, 33–54. New York: Taplinger, 1980.

The Illustrated Man

Fabun, Don. "Science Fiction—News from the Hinter Worlds." Review of *The Illustrated Man*. *San Francisco Chronicle*, 25 March 1951, 18.

Hoffman, Preston. Review of *The Illustrated Man* (audio version). *Wilson Library Bulletin* (May 1995): 95.

Review of *The Illustrated Man. Emergency Librarian* (January–February 1988): 22.
Review of *The Illustrated Man. Magazine of Fantasy and Science Fiction* (October 1997): 41–42.

Fahrenheit 451

Hoffman, Preston. Review of *Fahrenheit 451* (audio version). *Wilson Library Bulletin* (November 1994): 127.

Hoskinson, Kevin. "*The Martian Chronicles* and *Fahrenheit 451*: Ray Bradbury's Cold War Novels." *Extrapolation* 36, no. 4 (1995): 345–59.

McGiveron, Rafeeq O. "Bradbury's *Fahrenheit 451*." *Explicator* 54, no. 3 (1996): 177–80.

———. " 'Do You Know the Legend of Hercules and Antaeus?' The Wilderness in Ray Bradbury's *Fahrenheit 451*." *Extrapolation* 39, no. 2 (1997): 102–9.

———. " 'To Build a Mirror Factory': The Mirror and Self-Examination in Ray Bradbury's *Fahrenheit 451*." *Critique* 39, no. 3 (Spring 1998): 282–87.

———. "What 'Carried the Trick'? Mass Exploitation and the Decline of Thought in Ray Bradbury's *Fahrenheit 451*." *Extrapolation* 37, no. 3 (1996): 245–56.

Pober, Stacy. Review of *Fahrenheit 451* (audio version). *Library Journal* (July 1992): 146.

Seed, David. "The Flight from the Good Life: *Fahrenheit 451* in the Context of Postwar American Dystopias." *Journal of American Studies* [Great Britain] 28, no. 2 (1994): 225–40.

Trout, Paul A. "*Fahrenheit 451*: The Temperature at Which Critics Chill." *Cresset* (November 1993): 6–10.

Watt, Donald. "Burning Bright: *Fahrenheit 451* as Symbolic Dystopia." In *Ray Bradbury*, edited by Martin Harry Greenberg and Joseph D. Olander, 195–213. New York: Taplinger, 1980.

Dandelion Wine

Biddison, L. T. "Ray Bradbury's Song of Experience." *New Orleans Review* 1 (1979): 226–29.

Bowen, Robert O. "Summer of Innocence." Review of *Dandelion Wine. Saturday Review*, 7 September 1957, 18.

Mengeling, Marvin E. "Ray Bradbury's *Dandelion Wine*: Themes, Sources, and Styles." *English Journal* 60 (1971): 877–87.

Review of *Dandelion Wine. Kirkus Reviews*, 15 April 1957, 314.

Review of *Dandelion Wine. Magazine of Fantasy and Science Fiction*, October 1997, 89.

Rivette, Mark. "A Hot, Sunny Town in the Summer of '28." Review of *Dandelion Wine. San Francisco Chronicle*, 10 November 1957, 25.

Rosenman, John B. "The Heaven and Hell Archetype in Faulkner's 'That Evening

Sun' and Bradbury's *Dandelion Wine.*" *South Atlantic Bulletin* 43, no. 2 (1978): 12–16.

Skow, John. "The Summer of '28." Review of *Dandelion Wine. Time,* 24 March 1975, 78.

Taylor, G. Review of *Dandelion Wine. English Journal* 55 (1966): 614.

Something Wicked This Way Comes

De La Torre, Lillian. "Nightmare Unlimited." Review of *Something Wicked This Way Comes. New York Times Book Review,* 4 November 1962, 54.

Diskin, Lahna F. Review of *Something Wicked This Way Comes. Science Fiction and Fantasy Book Review,* October 1983, 18.

Review of *Something Wicked This Way Comes. New Yorker,* 27 October 1962, 216.

Touponce, William F. "Laughter and Freedom in Ray Bradbury's *Something Wicked This Way Comes.*" *Children's Literature Association Quarterly* 13, no. 1 (Spring 1988): 17–21.

Death Is a Lonely Business

Barber, Paul. Review of *Death Is a Lonely Business. Los Angeles Times Book Review,* 17 November 1985, 1.

Easton, Tom. Review of *Death Is a Lonely Business. Analog* September 1987, 159–60.

Kanfer, Stefan. "Dwarfed by Ancient Archetypes." Review of *Death Is a Lonely Business. Time,* 28 October 1985, 90.

Review of *Death Is a Lonely Business. Kirkus Reviews,* 15 August 1985, 799.

Review of *Death Is a Lonely Business. Publishers Weekly,* 23 August 1985, 63.

Review of *Death Is a Lonely Business. West Coast Review of Books,* November 1985, 30.

Sibley, Brian. "Cold Confection." Review of *Death Is a Lonely Business. Books and Bookmen,* June 1986, 36.

Graveyard for Lunatics

Annichiarico, Mark. Review of *A Graveyard for Lunatics. Library Journal,* 15 June 1990, 132.

Catling, Patrick Skene. "The Return of the Beast." Review of *A Graveyard for Lunatics. Spectator,* 6 October 1990, 29.

Hecklinger, Peggy. Review of *A Graveyard for Lunatics. School Library Journal* 36 (1990): 135.

Kanfer, Stefan. "Figments." Review of *A Graveyard for Lunatics. Time,* 6 August 1990, 75.

Kessel, John. "The Phantom of the Back Lot." Review of *A Graveyard for Lunatics*. *Los Angeles Times Book Review*, 5 August 1990, 8.

Review of *A Graveyard for Lunatics*. *West Coast Review of Books* 15, no. 6 (1990): 20.

Walz, Jim. Review of *A Graveyard for Lunatics*. *Book Report* (January-February 1991): 45.

Green Shadows, White Whale

Cook, Bruce. "Ray Bradbury and the Irish." *Catholic World* 200 (1965): 224–30.

Kanfer, Stefan. "Year of Living Dangerously." Review of *Green Shadows, White Whale*. *Time*, 25 May 1992, 68–69.

King, Francis. "In Search of the Great White Film Director." Review of *Green Shadows, White Whale*. *Spectator*, 17 October 1992, 30–31.

Review of *Green Shadows, White Whale*. *Kirkus Reviews*, 15 March 1992, 337.

Review of *Green Shadows, White Whale*. *Publishers Weekly*, 6 April 1992, 52.

OTHER SECONDARY SOURCES

Barry, Peter. *Beginning Theory: An Introduction to Literary and Cultural Theory*. Manchester, U.K.: Manchester University Press, 1995.

Booker, M. Keith. *Dystopian Literature: A Theory and Research Guide*. Westport, Conn.: Greenwood, 1994.

Bressler, Charles E. *Literary Criticism: An Introduction to Theory and Practice*. 2nd ed. Upper Saddle River, NJ: Prentice Hall, 1999.

Clute, John, and Peter Nicholls. *The Encyclopedia of Science Fiction*. New York: St. Martin's, 1993.

Cowan, Tom, and Jack Maguire. *Timelines of African-American History: 500 Years of Black Achievement*. New York: Berkley, 1994.

Davis, Robert Con and Ronald Schleifer. *Contemporary Literary Criticism: Literary and Cultural Studies*. 3rd ed. New York: Longman, 1994.

Fokkema, Douwe, and Elrud Ibsch. *Theories of Literature in the Twentieth Century*. New York: St. Martin, 1995.

Fuss, Diana. *Inside/Out: Lesbian Theories, Gay Theories*. New York: Routledge, 1992.

Greenblatt, Stephen, and Giles Gunn. *Redrawing the Boundaries: The Transformation of English and American Literary Studies*. New York: Modern Language Association, 1992.

Harmon, William, and C. Hugh Holman. *A Handbook to Literature*. 7th ed. Upper Saddle River, N.J.: Prentice Hall, 1996.

Hawthorn, Jeremy. *A Concise Glossary of Contemporary Literary Theory*. 2nd ed. London: Edward Arnold, 1994.

Hirschfelder, Arlene, and Martha Kreipe de Montano. *The Native American Almanac*. New York: Prentice Hall, 1993.

Morrison, Toni. *Playing in the Dark: Whiteness and the Literary Imagination*. Cambridge: Harvard University Press, 1992.

Sedgewick, Eve Kosovsky. *Between Men: English Literature and Male Homosocial Desire*. New York: Columbia University Press, 1985.

Tarbert, Gary. *Book Review Index*. Detroit: Gale Research, 1973-June 1996.

Wonham, Henry B. *Criticism and the Color Line: Desegregating American Literary Studies*. New Brunswick, N.J.: Rutgers University Press, 1996.

Index

murder mysteries, 88; plot development, 88–91; postmodern reading,
96–98; publishing history, 87;
setting, 95; themes, 95–96
Driving Blind, 19
Dystopias, 59–60

Faber, Professor (*The Illustrated Man*),
55, 57–58, 60
Fahrenheit 451, 13, 20–21, 53–62; charac-
ter development, 56; critical re-
sponse, 53; plot development, 54–56;
publishing history, 53–54; setting,
59; stylistic reading, 60–62; themes,
59–60
Feminist Analysis, 84–86
Finn, Heeber (*Green Shadows, White
Whale*), 110, 111, 116, 118–19
Foley, Miss (*Something Wicked This
Way Comes*), 75–78, 81, 86
Foucault, Michel, 96–97
Fury, Tom (*Something Wicked This
Way Comes*), 12, 74–75, 81

Gender Analysis, 70–72
The Golden Apples of the Sun, 15, 17, 50
A Graveyard for Lunatics, 1, 2, 4, 12, 22–
23, 88, 99–107; autobiographical
narrator, 99, 102–3; character development, 102–3; critical response, 99;
plot development, 100–102; publishing history, 99; relationship to
Death Is a Lonely Business, 99; semiotic reading, 106–7; setting, 104;
themes, 105–6
Green Shadows, White Whale, 4, 23, 88,
109–119; autobiographical narrator,
115–16; character development, 115–
16; critical response, 109; plot
development, 110–14; queer reading, 117–19; themes, 116–17
Green Town, 6, 69, 74; *Graveyard*, 100.
See also Waukegan

Halloway, Charles (*Something Wicked
This Way Comes*), 74, 77–80, 81, 85
Halloway, Mrs. (*Something Wicked
This Way Comes*), 82, 85–86
Halloway, William (Will) (*Something
Wicked This Way Comes*), 74–80, 81–
82, 83, 85
Harryhausen, Ray, 2, 22, 103. *See also*
Holdstrom, Roy
Heinlein, Robert, 2
Henry (*Death Is a Lonely Business, A
Graveyard for Lunatics*): *Death*, 93;
Graveyard, 99, 103, 105
Holdstrom, Roy (*A Graveyard for Luna-
tics*), 22, 100–101, 102, 103. *See also*
Harryhausen, Roy
Huff, John (*Dandelion Wine*), 65
Huston, John, 4, 23; *Green Shadows,
White Whale*, 110–11, 113–16

The Illustrated Man, 20, 37–51; character development, 39–44; plot development, 38–39; publishing history,
37–38; "race" in science fiction, 48–
51; settings, 44–47; themes, 47–48
I Sing the Body Electric!, 17

Leiber, Manny (*A Graveyard for Luna-
tics*), 100, 102, 103
Long After Midnight, 18
Los Angeles Science Fiction League, 2

Machineries of Joy, 17
The Martian Chronicles, 4, 19–20, 25–
35, 50; character development, 28–
32; critical response, 33; narrative
point of view, 28; plot development, 26–28; postcolonial reading,
34–35; publishing history, 25–26;
setting, 32–33; themes, 33–34
McClellan, Clarisse (*The Illustrated
Man*), 54, 57
McClure, Marguerite Susan, 3

About the Author

ROBIN ANNE REID is Assistant Professor of Literature and Languages at Texas A&M University–Commerce, Texas. She is the author of *Arthur C. Clarke: A Critical Companion* (Greenwood, 1997), as well as several articles on science fiction. Her other scholarly interests include feminist and multicultural literary theory and *Star Trek*. She writes poetry and fiction.

Critical Companions to Popular Contemporary Writers
Second Series

Rudolfo A. Anaya *by Margarite Fernandez Olmos*

Maya Angelou *by Mary Jane Lupton*

Louise Erdrich *by Lorena L. Stookey*

Ernest J. Gaines *by Karen Carmean*

John Irving *by Josie P. Campbell*

Garrison Keillor *by Marcia Songer*

Jamaica Kincaid *by Lizabeth Paravisini-Gebert*

Barbara Kingsolver *by Mary Jean DeMarr*

Terry McMillan *by Paulette Richards*

Larry McMurtry *by John M. Reilly*

Toni Morrison *by Missy Dehn Kubitschek*

Chaim Potok *by Sanford Sternlicht*

Amy Tan *by E. D. Huntley*

Anne Tyler *by Paul Bail*

Leon Uris *by Kathleen Shine Cain*

Critical Companions to Popular Contemporary Writers
First Series—*also available on CD-ROM*